HOT

& HEAVY

FIERCE FAT GIRLS ON LIFE, LOVE & FASHION

edited by Virgie Tovar

SEAL PRESS

HOT & HEAVY
Fierce Fat Girls on Life, Love & Fashion

© 2012 Virgie Tovar

Published by
Seal Press
A Member of the Perseus Books Group
1700 Fourth Street
Berkeley, California

Library of Congress Cataloging-in-Publication Data

Tovar, Virgie, 1982-
Hot & heavy : fierce fat girls on life, love & fashion / Virgie Tovar. — 1st ed.
p. cm.
ISBN 978-1-58005-438-6
1. Overweight women. 2. Body image in women. 3. Self-esteem in women.
I. Title. II. Title: Hot and heavy.
RC628.T682 2012
613.2'5—dc23
2012010730

9 8 7 6 5 4 3 2 1

Cover and interior design by Domini Dragoone
Cover photo © Carlos Batts
Cover model: April Flores
Interior photos: pages 11, 95, and 179 © Substantia Jones, www.SubstantiaJones.com; page 229 © Girl Crimson, http://girlcrimson.blogspot.com; and page 247 © Shilo McCabe | www.ShiloMcCabe.com.

Printed in the United States of America
Distributed by Publishers Group West

Dedicated to all of the fat girls
who feel they must apologize

And to all of those who don't

CONTENTS

PART 2
LOVE

PART 3
FASHION

Introduction

Virgie Tovar

I was born into a world where fat women are outlaws: a band of lawless revolutionaries, fighting against myopic standards of beauty and archaic forms of femininity. A world where fat women are like Che Guevara meets RuPaul, like Thelma and Louise meets Madonna—the stuff of fantasies and legends. We are the eaters of the crème brûlée and the tiramisu. We are the cupcake warriors, the sensualists, the plus-size queens. We are flag-bearers in a turgidly anti-pleasure society.

Fat is a delicious, cute, little word. The *f* and the *a* slip off the tongue as if they were dipped together in melty mascarpone. And the hard *t* at the end reminds you that there's a little punch to whomever is graced with the title. Oddly, the f-word is used to scare women, but it doesn't scare me. My fat is political because when I show it off it really seems to piss people off. My fat is political because I'm keeping it. My fat is political because it's fucking hot. My fat is my flag, my claim to fame, my battle scar, my secret fat girl society badge.

I live in a time of unprecedented freedom for women, the daughter borne of immigrant dreams and feminist fantasies. I have the freedom to own a company, terminate a pregnancy, remain fabulously single, and yet my freedom to be fat is heavily contested by my government, my community, my television set. As this book was written and edited, the War on Obesity had created a platform for polemicists to comment on the immorality of fat parents and for scientists to describe the alleged dumbing effects of fat on the brain.

As Don Kulick and Anne Meneley succinctly stated in *Fat: The Anthropology of an Obsession*, "It isn't just a chemical or biological fact. It is also a supremely cultural fact." Discussions of fat people, especially women, become texts, documents, artifacts that we must dissect, analyze, and explore. As the deeply flawed public health sector decries fatness as a medical pathology, an epidemic that threatens the Western world, we can hear the familiar sounds of an age-old reminder: "be good."

In the face of such platitudinous admonitions stands a bunch of big-ass, mouthy fat girls who wear fuchsia and feathers, who walk out in the world with bellies exposed and middle fingers raised. Take heed. Our bodies, our attitudes belie the polemics, unveil the truth: that being good doesn't get you much besides the title. Our day in the sun is only as far as we make it. And for girls willing to forsake good, there is deliciousness of a different kind to be had.

In soliciting submissions for *Hot & Heavy*, I asked fierce, fabulous women to tell the stories of how exactly they came to be that way. This thing called "fierce" is a single word meant to capture an infinite number of possibilities. It is not a single destination arrived at through the same infallible process. In my life, fierce looks like pencil skirts and cleavage, burlesque stardom and satin sheets. But we each decide what this word means to us. We do fierce the way that we do fierce. And what you're about to read are the ways that thirty-one women walk in fierce fatness. One for every day of the month.

When I conceived of the idea for this book, I thought, "This will be my chance to show the world how hot and amazing and fabulous fat girl life can be." And as with any project of fabulous-making, I secretly sought to hide the stories that complicate what fabulous really is. As a burlesque performer, I can tell you that fabulous looks flawless. When we're on stage, no hair seems out of place, no sequin seems amiss. When we're backstage, we are madly sewing things onto other things and gluing stuff to other stuff, and we do this to create an experience of perfection for the audience. If we can be that for you, then some part of us can be perfect, too. We hold your expectations, and they nourish us.

Sometimes we need someone who is—to us—flawlessly fabulous to give us the strength to do the things that might change our lives forever. I wanted to show you that and only that, but as I talked with the women who contributed to this book and as I read their words, I knew that editing out the complexity would be dishonest.

So, no piece in this book presents the picture-perfect image of body love nor is any piece in this book a tale of what life at the end of fat hatred or body hatred looks like. There is no such thing as "perfection." There is no such thing as "the end." But for those willing to step out into the limelight, there are beautiful secrets no diet or measuring tape can possibly reveal.

Fierceness is complicated. Fabulous lives in this book: in the words about great joy and hot sex and deep love, about delicious meals and amazing outfits, but also in the words about frustration and pain and loss.

Fabulous is so much more than just the sequins.

It's easy to be a lot of things, but it's not easy to be a fabulous fat girl. So, you're an over-achiever! You like that little extra bit of attention, those envious glances, those moments of glory.

You're in the limelight. So, strike a pose.

PART 1

LIFE

Life—we are told—is what waits at the other end of a body transformation, a complete overhaul of the current self, the loss of our fat selves. We are taught to live in a counter-factual future that, somehow, never stops feeling just beyond our reach. We lose bits of life to these fantasies.

The truth? Life happens now, not fifteen or thirty or one hundred pounds from now. You can wear that bikini now. You can go on a date now. You can play in the ocean now. You can wear a ridiculous hat or a sparkly pink miniskirt now. You can travel now. You can dance in your underwear now. You can savor and gasp-with-delight while eating that double crème brie, that ganache-smothered chocolate cake, that succulent pulled pork with a side of pickled okra right now. You have permission not to waste another

hour on self-denial. There's no need to mourn the time you've lost,
unless you really want to. We make mistakes. Savor them because
they are truly what exist at the heart of who you have become and
who you will be. And even on the path to self-love, you will make
many, many more sweet mistakes all along the way. As my lover
says, "Take the crunchy with the smooth." I love life advice based
on peanut butter metaphors! Dedicate your remaining days to deliciousness, to sating your hungers, to trying on lipstick, to breathing
mindfully, to touching your skin, to taking bubble baths, to practicing your strut.

In this section, you will read about fat girls living loudly. You
might want to listen to this. . . .

Shiny, Sparkly Things

Erin Kilpatrick

I have always been fat. I will always be fat, and I'm okay with that. There's a picture of me when I was a little girl in a Super Girl bikini, with arms reaching toward the sky, a round little-girl belly hanging out, and a smile that could rival the brightest summer day. I love that I am still that little girl inside, only now I have my superhero moments mostly naked on stage. Well, along with a nerdy day job that affords me a whole assortment of extra sparkly costumes. Today, I'm like Lois Lane and Superman combined.

I am a fat burlesque performer. Before that, I was a fat belly dancer. And before that, I was a chubby poet raised by lesbians, with a really fabulous grandma who instilled in me a love of all shiny, sparkly things. I come from an artist family, but unlike my family I choose a career of crunching numbers by day to spend my nights engaging in activities that amuse and delight me. It's kind of awesome that I lead a secret double life.

I'd be blowing smoke if I didn't acknowledge that being a fat girl in love with the stage has been, at times, a pain-in-the-ass journey fraught with dismissive and downright hateful people. But I like to think witnessing the spectacular fuckups and misadventures of another person can sometimes illuminate the way for someone who may feel themselves lost or directionless. Besides, life is no fun when we pretend it's rainbows and unicorns all the time. So this is the story of how I became body positive.

You could say that my life has been a little different. I mean everyone's life is different, but I was raised in a log cabin with a backyard of organic gardens, fruit trees, and edges of woodland and wilderness. It was not one's standard sort of family, but it worked for me. I was also a fat kid who moved around a lot growing up, so flack about my body was a given, an ever-oncoming background noise.

My mother was pretty supportive of all my childhood girlie tomboyishness. She never discouraged me from being the fattest girl in jazz class or at tap dancing lessons or playing GI Joes with the boys in the neighborhood. For as butch as she is, she still cannot figure out how something so femme came out of her body. She humored me for the most part, even through my pre-teen, pink-haired, mopey poetry-writing phase.

Being a fat girl with purple hair in yearbook, newspaper, band, *and* drama, I was quite accustomed to load-balancing over-commitments. So I spent my last two years of high school in college because that was the fashionable thing for angsty fat alternative teens to do. I got to indulge in classes in astronomy, figure drawing, and philosophy . . . and explain basic quantum physics to my typing class. It was wonderful.

Plus, I had pretty teenage punk boys in my Film As Literature class who didn't give two shits about my dress size. I ended up dating the grumpy one who colored my hair red on Valentine's Day and infused my music collection with punk and ska. I gave him a blue Mohawk, and he brought me flowers once a week at my crappy mall job.

For all the cups of diner coffee, matching combat boots, and hot teenage car sex, diverging ideas of growing up were causing us strife. We had the kind of fight that leaves a rift of silence between two people who love, and fight, and fuck, and do everything else with a deeply invested sense of passion.

> *"You'd better not take it for granted anymore. I'm not*
> *taking nothing for granted anymore."*

There are a million ways my life would be different if I had picked up the phone. Instead I paused in the doorway and let the tears fall as the answering machine apologies echoed through an empty house. I took a deep breath and let the door click shut behind me.

Rolling down the highway, I thought of all the things I wanted to say, all the things I couldn't say.

I saw the old white car swerve in the lane in front of me. I saw the van on the right shoulder, people behind it changing a tire. I saw the big red pickup truck with no driver, crossing the center lane. I put both feet on the brakes and held onto the steering wheel, willing my car to stop with everything in me.

It took less than a second. The screeching breaks, the smell of burning rubber, and the sound of a very large aluminum can smashed full force with a baseball bat . . . times a thousand. When I opened my eyes, I was bleeding onto the dashboard behind the steering wheel. Thick red plops from a cool wet fire spreading across my forehead. I saw wisps of smoke breathing through the cracks in the shattered windshield, curling in the sunlight like incense tendrils. Tempered glass glittered across the passenger seat, tangled with embroidery thread spools every color of the rainbow thrown forward from the back seat.

I tried to move, but one arm was pinned between my tummy and a broken steering wheel. The other was trapped behind it, locked in tight by the caved plastic and twisted metal that used to be the driver's side door. Both feet were still on the brake pedal, pushed back by the crash inertia that put the engine on my lap.

The floor had crumpled like an accordion beneath my knees. The dashboard rested on the shifter beside me. I was trapped in a metal cocoon, body pressed by metal on all edges, as growing flames lapped beyond the mangled windshield.

I thought I was fucked. A Bad Religion song played surreal on the slowing tape deck, singing "you'd better not take it for granted anymore; I'm not taking nothing for granted anymore." I felt burning at the tips of my toes, flowing up over my skin to the top of my head. I tilted my head back and started screaming.

I didn't see my life flash before me nor did I see Jesus. I am eternally grateful to the people driving behind me who carried a fire extinguisher and called 911. I am grateful to the police, fire, and rescue workers who spent the next two hours to use the Jaws of Life to extract me from my car. Even if they had to break all the windows and cut the roof off before lifting the engine off my chubby lap. Even if they stabbed me multiple times trying to run an IV and kept asking the same questions over and over. Even if they never seemed to actually call my mom, no matter how many times I gave them my phone number. I am grateful to all the people on the road that day who prayed for me.

When I was airlifted to the hospital, I cried.

The emergency room of a trauma center is a scary place. I mean, not only was I naked, covered in glass and blood and car guts with my neck braced, but the rest of me was strapped to a back board. A drunk in the next bed over was causing all sorts of crashing, screaming "get your fucking hands off me," adding to the chaotic emergency-room ambiance. A lot of people worked on me that day, poking me with tiny cameras to inspect my innards, scraping dried blood and car shrapnel off my face, and finally X-raying and then re-X-raying me after all my piercings were removed.

I spent one sleepless night in the neurological ward with no good drugs or anyone surrendering to my pleas to order pizza. I hope to never spend another night in a hospital. Being lucid in a trauma ward is an intense mish-mash of screaming through-out the night, metered by the soft squeak of squishy white nurse shoes. Every cell in me ached with a soreness and nightmares I had never known.

The next morning, I totally had a Blair moment—from that episode of *Facts of Life* where she gets a scratch across her forehead from a car accident, then holds up the food tray as a mirror with one shaking hand, and cries that she will never be pretty again. I had to laugh at myself. I think I played that out in my head to stave off realities of sitting in a hospital chair in a shower, washing dried blood, glass, and tufts of hair off my head with the one arm I could still lift. The nastiness of hospital soap mixed with the blood turned my hair from purple to gray.

Sitting there, I had a stark moment to assess my body. It looked like a map, bruise oceans crisscrossed with red scratch highways and lumps of newly formed swollen mountain ranges. There were large ridges of bruising across my lap. My left leg was a sea of pummeled blue from ankle to hip, with scabs forming solitary islands. My left arm so inky purple that only a thin islet of flesh color remained. Over the bruises were craters of embedded glass. My right forearm, also indigo, matched the two bruises on top and under my breast from the seatbelt. I had a deep crevasse of red from eyebrow to beyond my hairline. It was laced with smaller crimson streaks from the windshield. It was a horrible-beautiful landscape: traumatic, but survivable. My belly was an oasis of untouched softness.

When I couldn't stand on my own, the nurse made quite an escapade of forcing me to hobble unassisted with no sympathy for my moment of sore, freaked out, self-pity–induced helplessness. This was not something I was to surrender to; this was something I would rise above. Like a phoenix, a really clumsy, accident-prone phoenix. When my friends came to visit me in the hospital, I had to show them how badass I was. I flung the sheets back and showed them how amazing my bruises were. I had survived.

"You're lucky you were carrying a little extra weight, or you wouldn't be standing here."

The doctor asked if my car had an airbag. He was in disbelief at the demise of my old Honda at the hands of a brand new full-size Dodge Ram pickup truck. The driver had leaned over to fiddle with the cruise control and crossed the centerline. I left 54 feet of skid marks between hitting the brakes and impact. I was stopped and he hit me head-on going 65 miles per hour. He never even saw me.

The doctor watched me negotiate a few hallway stairs, then discharged me to the trauma center with blessings and ibuprofen. I walked (slowly) out of the hospital the day after the accident. It was called a miracle. I know I was fucking lucky, maybe even graced with a second chance.

No broken bones. No internal bleeding. While I would not advocate going through a horrific crash to realign one's body priorities, that accident really changed how I looked at life. Not just in the lottery-style up-on-my-accident-karma kind of way, but it also disabled my ability to truly hate on my body. My body saved me. And more specifically, my fat saved me. If I had been skinny, I likely wouldn't be here to tell my story. That was a pretty profound moment for my eighteen-year-old self.

Before that, my body and I got along, but we weren't what you would call "close." Afterward, especially given all the recovery, I just could not deny myself a little body care and compassion. And pool time with the fat old ladies. And a bunch of herbal poultices because, as previously mentioned, I lived in a queer, pro-herbal-medicine household.

A few years after all the doctors and chiropractors and all the medical bills were paid, I started dancing.

The first time I performed burlesque, I literally had nude leggings under nude pantyhose under nude fishnets under regular fishnets, and a corset, and a body stocking. People loved me anyway, even if I had a moment of body insecurity. It took me a few years to become entirely comfortable with my relative nakedness on stage. But the only way to get better is to be on stage, and the only way to truly let go of one's inhibitions is to be fabulous in the face of fear.

I never took a class in burlesque, per se. I joined a troupe and started performing. We performed at fund-raisers and festivals, supporting a body-positive politic by actually putting different bodies on stage. Because of the people I was performing with, I got a crash course in making politics visible. We did acts about food, we did acts as a commentary on beauty standards, and we did acts that were campy and silly and gay. We had dialogues about integrating anti-oppression into our work and on how to best tackle body negativity in performance. We talked about art as activism. Activism as action. It was like a whole new sparkly world of awesomeness.

I've seen troupes come and go and I've seen the community shift and change as these things tend to do. I have been extremely lucky in my experiences. Burlesque has led me to some of the most fabulously rhinestoned, politically kick-ass people I have ever come across. It leads me into (sometimes uncomfortable) dialogues about body politics, fat politics, and owning your identity. I've learned to tackle being fat-positive by doing it fully engaged, with eyes open and while knowing what I stand for.

> *"I love seeing fat girls on stage. I think it's important to be a fat girl on stage."*

I'm not saying burlesque is without its own bullshit. There are venues in my city that have a "no fat girl" policy. I have no shame in telling people that's why I won't spend money there. As a reaction to it, I want to make a traveling road show of fat girls to tour across the country. I want to support new fat girls finding their stage wings and shaking their big girl bits. I still think the world is what you make it, and I want to do my part to show how awesome fat girls are.

I no longer wear a bunch of layers on stage. I don't hide my belly in corsets or even wear pantyhose. Hell, someday I may even graduate to a g-string. In the last year, I helped teach a room full of fat girls how to twirl pasties, I've seen my boobies across the big screen at a film festival, and I've been deemed the "Burlesque Costume MacGyver" in a room full of fat performers. I'm the fattest I've ever been, and I take off my clothes in public regularly. I never really thought I would end up here, but I'm the happiest I've ever been and I wouldn't change a thing. I am my own superhero, and I have a whole collection of scars, stories, and sparkly spandex costumes to prove it.

Fat at the Gym

Emily Anderson

In my pre-fat acceptance (PFA) life, I felt caught in the paradox of being fat at the gym: the fear that I didn't belong in its hallowed, sweaty halls, but if I didn't go, I would never become un-fat and finally worthy. While attending a college touted as one of the most physically fit in the country, I often watched thin pre-med majors race down treadmills, simultaneously annotating biology textbooks. They were so *in control*, so healthy and good in the eyes of a weight-obsessed college campus. My timid, embarrassed ventures into the gym were part of a regimen, written in tiny print in a tiny notebook in my attempts to become un-fat. These adventures involved fleeing the weight room when male friends came in to lift and plenty of guilt on days I skipped.

My journey to fat acceptance is full of sad nights, drunk-crying that I wasn't beautiful, with an implied belief that my worth was tied to being seen as sexually desirable and conquerable to the average equally drunk male at the bar. My journey frequently mirrored traditional tales of dieting and gaining and dieting again, being praised for "looking so good" when I lost weight, and feeling hateful toward my body when it returned to its natural form.

And it ended—or began, truly—when I realized I was valuable as a person, not despite my body, but *for* my body and my personhood and my laughter and for all of me. In almost a serendipitous manner, all of the fat- and body-positive literature I had been reading, the blogs I followed, and the pictures of beautiful fat people I admired clicked in my head, and knowledge became acceptance. If my interest in someone wasn't returned, I no longer feared that I was flawed. My negative egoism, my obsessive disparaging of my own worth evaporated.

So with newfound courage and bravery I walked into a gym again, this time as a fatty who loved her fat and wasn't trying to undo her body, or to become un-fat.

Being a fat woman at the gym is in itself an act of social disobedience. I shouldn't be in there, taking up the space of the lithe-bodied, unless it's with a face of sincere penance and shame. But I have claimed the gym as my own. I celebrate being visible and fat all over the gym—running and sweating and sometimes breaking into song, lifting dumbbells alongside muscle-laden men with uncompleted tribal band bicep tattoos, flinging my weight around in aerobics, and finally cooling it poolside in my bright, non-apple-body-shape flattering tankini. I smile and chat with women before yoga and mention how hungry I always am after class and can't wait to eat. I want to be seen. I am fat and happy in places where I should be fat and shameful, and denying this stereotype is a political action in my eyes.

I experience the transgressive thrill of exercising without the intention or effort to lose weight every time I scan my membership card at the entrance. A thin friend of mine, who typically eats little and exercises often, recently went with me to my gym. She asked me how much weight I was trying to lose, if I was dieting again like I had in college. The words "I don't want to lose any weight" sent chills of excitement up and down my spine and provoked mostly a loss of words from her. There's an adrenaline rush that comes with denying the common rules of society: that I should always be trying to lose weight, that I should always be unhappy with some flaw. To say I am perfectly content with my body and all the parts that assemble it is nothing less than radical.

I attempt to make my disinterest in losing weight as frequent in conversation as the constant bemoaning of losing just ten more, five more, some more pounds with which I am inundated by friends, advertising, and passing acquaintances. I've searched for new phrases to say when someone tells me they're starting a diet or trying to lose weight. PFA, I would have applauded them and deprecated myself, the socially approved standard response to weight-loss goals. Now, I can only offer up a watery "that's nice" and send glowing love to my big thighs.

But my most transgressive and transformative action came simply and without expectations of the ramifications it would have for my fat acceptance. I was running on the elliptical machine, absorbed in my breathing, music filling my ears, when *the act* occurred. Until this very moment on a Friday afternoon, if sweat was coating my face I would pull up on the neck of my shirt. Often it was already darkened with a rapidly cooling saturation of sweat, ineffectual for satisfactory drying. I had an idea, but it was daring and bold and I wasn't sure if I was ready. Then, recklessly, I did it. I lifted the hem of my T-shirt, exposing my round belly, complete with the light pink trails of stretch marks across its nearly fluorescent white skin, to wipe my sweaty face while running.

A simple, common action for the typical gym goer, at least the one who doesn't pack a travel bag complete with face towel. Something so natural as to bring that cotton fabric up to my face—I'm wearing my own towel. But years and years of experience had trained me to keep that hem a few inches below the waist of my shorts. This hem-to-waist observation followed me from being a mini-fat in pre-adolescence dance classes, to a teenage fat careful of stretching too far back during school, to a college fat who worked out at the gym in a haze of apology for forcing others to watch me attempt to become un-fat.

PFA training be damned. I wiped my face with the hem of my shirt, and the floodgates of visible fat pride were opened. The feeling of cool air on my belly, hanging over my gym shorts for the world to see was intoxicating. Here, T-shirts were the first to be sacrificed. They quickly lost their arms, their sides, and ribbed necks to become breezy, cut-away tank tops. My side fat, my upper arms, the indentations my sports bra presses into my pillowy ribcage, on display. Shirts I lift and lower like fat pride flags.

I bought skintight exercise tanks that stretched across my belly with the gentle sensuality of kid gloves from a Victorian romance novel. But my romance was not with a rogue dandy, but with my own belly outline. The wonderfully circular indentation of my belly button, a miniature mysterious cave in the front of my body, points inward to my gut.

Then came the tiny shorts. These tiny shorts, which appeared to be a pair of boyshort underwear with a bedazzled waistband sewn to the top, were absorbed into my wardrobe until they replaced all the baggy netted basketball shorts with smooth spandex. They became my flag of fatass pride. The first time I wore them through the lobby of the gym, I was overwhelmed by the sheer deviant pleasure of it. Did other people see this? Did they see how tight these tiny shorts were, how my thighs showed and rubbed and touched each other as I walked, how perfectly encased in stretchy cotton my ass was? I was titillated by the shamelessness of these tiny shorts. I brandished my fat legs at fellow gym goers, my weapons of love and acceptance.

There is, to the best of my knowledge, no secret handshake for happy fats at the gym. I often gaze sideways at other fat people in the gym, sweating over the cross-trainers or curling their dimply knees toward their chests, and wonder who else isn't trying to join the ranks of un-fattening. Short of wearing an "ask me about my fat acceptance" button on the front of my sports bra, I am unsure how to convey this to others around me. Because I *want* to talk about it with everyone—the older woman I consider my fat-at-the-gym hero, who does so many shoulder presses that she blazes with strength, and the fat man who arrives at the exact same time as me at the elliptical machines every afternoon with such regularity that I internally refer to him as my gym boyfriend. But most of all, the quiet, timid fat teen girls who slink up to the machines like they want to disappear. I know what it's like to think you don't belong in the gym, to look around and see bodies that are so different than yours, bodies you are supposed to aspire toward.

For those girls, I wear tiny shorts and wipe my sweat with the bottom of my shirt. I run and I breathe so loudly, big noisy gulps of air. I dance a little on the elliptical and break into song and can't always contain my fist pumps. The gym should be a place of pleasure. I do everything I can to show how much joy I'm taking in exercise, and in my own body. If I become that fat woman who won't stop singing along to Beyoncé while she's running, I'll also be that fat woman who looks so sincerely happy while she's running—happy in a place where she's supposed to be self-flagellating.

I expose my body to expose the fears of others—the fear of claiming space as a fat person, the fear of calling attention to a body outside the bounds of accepted perfection. The other day, I saw another fat woman in tiny shorts on the treadmill ahead of me—tiny shorts, the secret handshake of happy fats.

Together, we're accomplishing so much more than burning calories.

Public Stretch Mark Announcement

Emma Corbett-Ashby (Goldie Dartmouth)

I recently debuted a new fat-positive performance of mine called Public Stretch Mark Announcement in Berlin (Germany), where I live. The show involves my reading out a spoken word piece about stretch marks and includes a partially animated stretch-mark slide-show. I wear a revealing bikini and invite the audience to come and examine my stretch marks.

There has been a fat activist group called *Dicke* present in Berlin for a number of years, but so far the only specifically fat-positive performance events in Berlin have been produced by me. I hope that this will change, and I feel optimistic that it will, what with a fat-positive conference coming up and growing momentum around the issue in Europe.

When considering fat positivity, it's worth remembering that all might not be as it is in your vicinity. There are some parts of the world where I've been lucky enough to visit, where fat-positive performance and fat bodies on stage are regular parts of the land-scape. It's almost a given, which is a great thing. I have a good community of fat-positive folks in other parts of the world, and interestingly in the longtime fat activists I'm starting to recognize a certain vibe of "I've been doing this fat-positive thing for so long, I'm kinda over it," not in the sense that it's no longer important, but just in the sense that it's no longer a huge focus or a huge point of discussion. It's achieved. It's done. It's great when people feel this way. What better circumstance than a situation where fat positivity is normal?

I sometimes find myself thinking this way also. My daily battle in front of the mirror and my daily critical appraisal of my stomach in the shower or my thighs in jeans are certainly far, far behind me. But this blissful state doesn't continue for long. There are just too many reminders that the vast majority of the world has yet to catch up—not only on the streets (and don't even get me started about the amount of fatphobic street harassment that exists in my neighborhood) but also in the performer/audience circles, in Berlin and elsewhere. Despite the growing celebration of fatter girls on stage, especially if they're curvy and not wearing much, the sight of brazen, all-out fat is still contested. And I think this is something about skin.

Fatties know skin. Something I remember hearing as a child from a well-meaning adult, who no doubt thought they were very kind, was that fat people are lucky because they have such beautiful creamy, smooth skin. Ha. I wonder if some people really do imagine and want fatties to be living, breathing Renaissance paintings, all carefully executed curves and perfect. Smooth. Skin. Renoir? The "master" of the glorified curvy ladies always gently braiding their hair or reclining by a riverside in the sunshine, you could call Renoir an early proponent of air brushing. In all those blurs and swirls of paint, no need to capture the stretch marks, right?

I've got stretch marks. I still discover them in places that I hadn't noticed, those telltale rivulets of skin, some already faded to blend in with the rest of me. My first batch I got during adolescence when I was sprouting all over the place, mainly down my inner thighs and also across my hips, which was a huge source of shame for me back then. To me, stretch marks meant fat-where-there-shouldn't-be-fat. The skin freaking out in protest: "What are you doooooooooing?? Don't leave the desired shape!" Later in life, in my thirties, I now have a fresh influx that are still multiplying. On my hips, but also my stomach, particularly my lower stomach, below my navel.

I remember one of my first lovers examining the marks on my hips and asking, "Are these scars?" I actually dearly wanted to pretend they were scars, from some exciting, sexy, dangerous occurrence, not just the side effects of a fat body. I think, as far as I recall, that I was too ashamed to admit what they were. I just avoided the question. If my lover really thought they were scars, I wonder what they imagined had caused them? Possibly the fictional thin person inside of me trying to claw her way out?

This isn't an isolated example, of course; many people without fat bodies still do not know what stretch marks are.

This was partly my inspiration behind the Public Stretch Mark Announcement performance. The name was a deliberate choice. It was descriptive, of course, but it was also deliberately referencing popular subversive performance art. Annie Sprinkle made the decision to exhibit her cervix as part of her performance art exhibit *Public Cervix Announcement* in 1990. She is well known for her work as a sex-positive educator, artist, and porn star. I enjoy her approach, and my critique is not aimed at her personally. She is a groundbreaking and powerful feminist performance artist. My critique, rather, is again quite location specific.

I have lived in Berlin for two and a half years. Part of the context for this performance was living in a city that is notorious for its art scene and all the elitism, exploitation, gentrification, and social exclusion that comes with that. There are many female performance artists in Berlin. With few exceptions, they are all slim women. A critique of this fact does not vilify individual performers; it is more aimed at a general atmosphere and the widely held expectation and values that a woman would not choose to exhibit her body in a high-art context if it was not something that met certain standards. It would almost be seen as having the nerve, the cheek to exhibit an imperfect body, to subject the public to it.

This attitude is also mirrored in other popular alternative media. I'm not even going to start on mainstream media; I guess I don't expect much from that. But "alternative" media purport to be an alternative. Just saying. The many local independent, arty, and queer magazines are full of slim people. Generally speaking, slim people who are also white. Among the other divisions of popular culture, from the DJs to the musicians, to the performers, to the porn actors, to the artsy kids, to the scene queens and kings who have somehow fostered notoriety and some degree of small-scale celebrity, the story is the same. They are all, almost without exception, slim.

This is a simplified overview; there are of course many other factors to be considered. For instance, the fact that many also fall into the categories of white, young, and hip, and of an elusive class of often English-speaking young people who have a great degree of mobility, both in terms of geography—where they can choose to live—and livelihood—with a seemingly invisible means of supporting themselves and plenty of time for glamorous party going and creative endeavors.

This is pretty much the same world in fashionable cities; it's not so exclusive to Berlin. But something about the particular Berlin-associated combination of self-conscious living-the-dream scenester-ism, elitism, and general ego-maniac's paradise drives me a bit crazy. This is only a part of what makes up this city, and a very small part at that. But unsurprisingly it's the part that garners the most attention: media, financial, and otherwise. I'm also just really tired of it. I apologize, slim performance art women. Some of your work is great. I'm just really tired of seeing smooth, lithe, delicately muscular bodies in the public sphere. I want to see stretch marks.

Oh yes, fatties know skin. We know stretch marks, we know broken capillaries, we know roughening, we know sweat rash, we know loose skin, we know cellulite and pimples. We know chafe. Oh god, we know chafe. I have chafed badly enough to have bleeding open wounds that took weeks to heal.

I love a fat body on stage, on the cover of a magazine, on TV, and in art. But though I love a fat silhouette, I also want to see some fat skin! Skin is where it starts to get controversial. It pushes the envelope. I will always remember a film lecturer saying to me that part of the reason that *Blue Velvet* was such a controversial film was because you could see Isabella Rosselini's cellulite.

Fat and our experience of it is more than size and weight alone. Fat is the relationship it has to your skin, to the casing of your body.

I've spoken to people about how my love of fatshion—I suspect many a fat girl's love of fatshion—is about the particular importance of the desire to feel comfortably and happily encased as a fat person. We don't need clothes that don't fit, are too tight, or are not designed for our bodies. That's the sort of thing that makes us feel wrong in our skin. Great outfits make us feel good in our bodies, which makes us carry ourselves with pride and pleasure. When people describe a person with an embodied presence and confident body language, they describe them as being comfortable in their own skin. This is something that I always seek to bring to the stage. I hope I appear comfortable in my own skin as a performer. Sometimes it's hard to know how comfortable I look because I definitely get nervous, which might affect my body language. But I hope being at ease in my skin comes across, and I also hope I can encourage the audience to feel at ease with my skin as well.

There is something very real, in terms of comfort zones, wherein fat is more acceptable if it has some tasteful, appropriate packaging—by that we're sort of back to the creamy smooth skin story. Smooth fat, without dimples or marked skin, properly epilated fat, sweet-smelling fat, reposed fat: properly attired in a tasteful, concealing manner. One of the reasons I get so into how Beth Ditto presents herself in concert is that she tends to fuck with all these rules. Beth Ditto goes for sweat, body hair, cellulite, and the whole deal. I saw a picture of her once in concert, and you could see her chafe. It was amazing. That's punk rock! Chafe is punk rock. Chafe was part of the performance, just as body hair and sweat marks were part of the performance. That's not to say that they were artificially engineered for that purpose, but that they were integral. Fat skin is fierce. Fat skin is evidence of a tangible, raw physicality that shows no fear.

Stretch marks are right behind this. My stretch marks are right behind this. Whatever they symbolize in people's minds (a flaw, the vulnerability of the limits of our bodies, a sign of a body that's "too much" or "let itself go," discomfort, shame, or damage), I want them to be given some reverence. Annie Sprinkle intended her Public Cervix Announcement to "lift the veil of ignorance" around the internal goings-on of a vagina. There was celebration and pride, but there was also empathy. Annie Sprinkle understood that people were likely to feel scared of her cervix. I myself also appreciate and understand that people have shame and fear around stretch marks. Someone I spoke to about the performance expressed so much shame about her own stretch marks that she looked like she might cry. Body shame runs deep. Even the most upbeat and self-loving fatties feel they're on shaky ground every now and then. Sometimes this stuff can surprise us and emerge from somewhere deep we thought was long behind us.

I had the privilege of hearing an idol of mine (who also happens to be fat), Dorothy Allison, the author of *Bastard Out of Carolina*, give a speech where she incorporated stretch marks into a story she wove about insecurity, feminine competition, and the struggle for solidarity when we get hit where it hurts. Her line was something like this: "Whoever you're with, they probably weren't your first choice. That skinnier, prettier, less stretch-marked bitch probably got the one you really wanted." Naturally this was satire, but it was also her way of playfully provoking her audience (largely made up of female identified people) to face ourselves.

Dorothy Allison (who, it goes without saying, could give many a "skinnier, prettier, less stretch-marked bitch" a run for their money) is ferocious partly due to her lack of fear in speaking the unspoken and delving into the depths of our universal fears and angst. We all know that deep, deep down, we have times when we feel unlovable. We feel inadequate. And our fat bodies with their stretch marks and cellulite and loose skin are a part of that. In fact, many women situate almost all of their unlovable feelings in their fat. It's okay to know this. There is no point in denying it. Use it as a guide and *own* it. Tough, nuanced women aren't afraid to go deep. Loving your body is empowering, but admitting to yourself that there are times when you don't and making your peace with that—this is what is true for most of us—is powerful on a whole other level. I also like to think of it as the oppositional pull to the empowerment we feel, making it stronger.

The performance was an intense experience, largely because witnessing people's shyness and discomfort with contested bodies is an intense thing, especially when that body is your own. Coaxing them out of this zone and creating a safe space was the challenge. But whatever I feel about my own stretch marks, however vulnerable, proud, fascinated or panicky they make me feel, I want them to be there and I want them to be seen. I want people to touch them, examine them, and in doing so empathize and connect with a part of me that rarely gets seen, and not just for the reason that it's below my knicker line. Publicly announced for what they are, I can't think of a better way to give them that space.

Take off the Damn Shoe!

Deah Schwartz

It's like the proverbial pebble in the shoe. It starts off as a small rattle. You are aware of something that you were previously unaware of. Where you once felt comfortable, suddenly you are feeling an irritation.

Time passes. You continue to go about your business, and the pebble starts to feel more like a rock. You take steps, and it digs into your foot. You try to navigate around it. You shake your foot. You favor the other foot. Finally, it is so disruptive, painful, and intrusive you have no choice but to stop what you are doing, sit down, and just take off the damn shoe. As you shake out the shoe, you are shaking your head in unison . . . why didn't you just do this sooner?

You put your shoe back on, and as you start to walk again you are expecting to be pain free, rock free, but it takes a while because there is bruising where the stone had been pushing into the sole of your foot for so long. And there is this strange sense memory of the rock that lingers even though you removed the actual cause of the problem. But eventually you realize that it's been a while since you were thinking about your foot, the rock, or the shoe. The memory grows dimmer, and you are just living your life.

I had no idea I was a fat kid until I was given the message from the people around me. I actually spent numerous hours, days, and years just living my life in concert with my body, mind, and spirit. I was happy and woke up in the mornings thinking about normal kid stuff like Rocky and Bullwinkle, buying new sneakers, and fighting with my sister. I did not wake up thinking about my body.

Once I was labeled as fat, cautioned that I shouldn't get any fatter, and warned that I would ruin my entire life if I didn't lose weight, everything changed. I started waking up in the morning and my first thoughts were that my body was wrong: how would I make it through the day with that body? My body became a separate entity. There was me and there was *that body*. I lived with a longing to be thin and the pain of *not* being thin. The discontent hardened and became a constant unwelcome rock in my shoe . . . a "sole-mate" (pun-groan) not of my choosing. As years passed, I lived my life constantly accommodating for the rock. No matter what my accomplishments were, they were eclipsed by my failure to attain the "look" of a successful woman. I always assumed that somehow the rock had the right to be where it was and I had to work around it.

For someone who has always hated being told to "be patient" and "wait," it is ironic how much of my life I spent putting my life on hold. It was subtle at first. The weather would start getting warmer and kids would start going to the community pool or the beach (I grew up in New York, not far from the Atlantic Ocean). I would watch enviously as they rode off on bikes loaded with towels headed for a day of splashing and swimming. I made up excuses: "When it gets warmer, I'll go." When it got warmer, I resorted to, "I have a cold" or "I get earaches from swimming."

Of course the real reason was how much I dreaded having to wear a bathing suit in public. When my excuses just didn't hold water, I yanked out the big gun: "I'm a redhead, and I'll just get sunburned." I wore a giant T-shirt over my hideous, black, one-piece bathing suit, explaining, when asked, "It is to protect me or I'll look like a lobster!" I tried with all of my might to stay out of sight. I put endless opportunities of having summer fun on hold because of my body-hate. I almost didn't graduate high school because of the swimming requirement in physical education. Putting my life on hold became part of how I operated in the world. "When I lose weight, then I will go to that party. When I lose weight, then I will take that class. When I lose weight, then Davey Bernstein will like me. When I lose weight, then I will really live the life I want to live."

How many kids are putting their lives on hold because they are being consumed by such shame and self-hate that they don't give themselves the opportunities to try things, to let go and dive in?

It never occurred to me to just take off the damn shoe.

It sounds so simple now. It wasn't. It took me years of therapy and self-exploration. There was no magic transformation. I still had to deal with the bruising and habits formed from years of living with what sometimes felt like a whole quarry of rocks in my shoe. Writing and performing in *Leftovers*, a show about eating disorders and fat acceptance made a difference. Eight shows a week, three of us took the stage, in leotards and tights, and sang about how beauty and success comes in all shapes and sizes. Joining like-minded communities and participating in educating others continues to reinforce and validate the choice I made.

When I was the director of the Expressive Arts Therapy Department at a psychiatric hospital in the Bay Area, there were many ways we categorized our patients. One way was to separate the voluntary admissions from the involuntary admissions. Along with the label *voluntary admit* came an assumption that this patient was ready to change. Conversely, the *involuntary admits* were being forced to change. In both cases, change was an elusive goal. In both cases, resistance was a formidable barrier to actualizing change. Even the voluntary patients with the internal desire to change bumped up against the walls of resistance.

Change is hard.

When a person embarks on the road of size acceptance, which may include changing their ways of eating or their relationship with food, it is often a result of external pressure to be different from what they are. They are being told over and over to change. "Change your diet. Change your body. Change your behavior. Change your appearance." The overriding message is, "You are not okay."

I worked with a patient once who told me, "If I ever kill myself, tell people it was because I couldn't stand facing another day looking in the mirror and starting the day off hating myself." She felt like a failure, every morning, because she couldn't change herself in the way that others wanted her to change. The only definition of change she could articulate or imagine was to change the way she looked to please her family. We worked on redefining her criteria for change. We looked at why others had the authority to prescribe *her* Change Menu. We looked at what she would change about herself if no one else had a say and she could just change what *she* wanted. We explored her resistance to change, inside and out.

One day in our Drama Therapy group, she announced that she was doing a scene about the two things she wanted to change about herself more than anything.

The group waited. Would it be her butt? Her thighs? Her upper arms?

Her scene was enthralling, powerful, humorous, and poignant. As the scene ended, she was in a restaurant. She ordered her selections from the Change Menu, "For my main course, I'll have the not giving my power of self-acceptance away to my family. And for dessert, I'll have the learning to speak Spanish fluently please." It's been a while since I've heard from this patient. But from time to time, I like to think of her sitting in a restaurant in Barcelona, speaking perfect Spanish and loving herself as she is.

As for the bathing suit, I think the first time I ever felt completely comfortable wearing a bathing suit was when I was pregnant and I had permission to be a fat woman in a bathing suit. The freedom I experienced was an indescribable joy. I remember at eight months pregnant I could feel my son swimming around inside of me as I was buoyantly bobbing around in the pool, completely unself-conscious, no big T-shirt, just sunscreen and a big grin on my face.

I vowed in that moment to do three things. First, whatever traces of negative feelings I still had about my body I would *not* put myself on hold. I would allow my kid to experience the joys of being a kid, even if it meant my wearing a bathing suit in public.

Second, whatever body shape, size, or type my child would develop, I would love him unconditionally and do what I could to help him foster love and acceptance for his body.

Third, and perhaps most challenging, I would take an active role in educating others about the damage that size discrimination inflicts on people. Sometimes, ironically enough, this means asking people to hold their tongues and open their minds.

My son is grown up now, and I am thrilled to say he has never put his life on hold, and I honestly can't remember the last time I did either.

Today my body is no longer a separate entity and I no longer open my eyes and greet the day with thoughts of hating my body. The memory of that pain has faded, and I am relieved to be walking forward, unencumbered.

The pebble is gone, and I'm just living my life.

To Be Seen

Kat Urice

I got my first job as an artist's model when I was eighteen, and it happened exactly the way you might imagine it would. A grungy, well-read–looking painter by the name of Clyde Steadman quite literally picked me out in a crowded bar (that I had snuck into with a fake ID and a group of friends), handed me his card with a practiced flourish, and asked if I would be interested in sitting for a painting. That was four years ago in 2008, and I've worked with various artists off and on since then, mostly painters, a couple of photographers, and occasionally I'll model for classes.

When I tell friends or acquaintances about this second job, their first reaction is usually shock. I am not a terribly extroverted person and, as one friend put it, taking your clothes off and standing up in front of an audience takes a certain amount of exhibitionism that you might not expect from me. I am also queer, and some find it strange that I would choose to expose my body to artists, the majority of whom are men. But mostly people just find it hard to believe that anyone would hire a fat girl as a model.

Most children are told that they can be anything they want to be. But for fat girls, this is simply not the case. It was made clear to me early on that certain occupations, such as ballerina, gymnast, actress, Hooters waitress, pop sensation, and model, are off limits. Those professions require that one be objectifiable for the satisfaction of the all-seeing proverbial gaze, and the gaze takes no pleasure in looking at fat. Before I started modeling, that was how I saw myself: a grotesque sexless elephant in the room. I didn't want to be seen, and I was under the impression that no one wanted to see me. So when Clyde Steadman approached me that night, I thought he must be joking because it was simply unimaginable that he would be genuinely interested in recreating my likeness.

Despite my fears and my better judgment, something compelled me to meet with him. It presented a unique opportunity to see myself as someone else saw me. So I skipped school the following week and took a bus downtown to meet Steadman at his studio. It was a third-floor walk-up in the Capitol Hill district, with a cold concrete floor and walls lined to the ceiling with books and impressionist renderings of baseball players, burlesque dancers, musicians, rubber ducks, and cattle. I tried to imagine myself among them and how I would look if rendered in that aesthetic.

At the center of the room sat a sagging blue futon and an easel. Steadman took up station behind his easel and started sketching while I sat on the too-low futon, feeling uncomfortable with my knees nearly bent to my chest. It was just like a regular job interview except his eyes kept flashing between me and the easel and all of his questions came out sounding distracted. He wanted to know how old I was. How much did I know about art? Was I in school? Where did I go? Did I have any vices? Did I eat meat? Was I planning to be a senator's wife? Almost mid-sentence Steadman bolted out of his chair and began rifling through his vast library of reference books. He said that ". . . skinny people, models, willing to take their clothes off are, like, a dime a dozen and frankly they got to be a bit boring."

The book he'd been searching for was on Lucian Freud. He opened it to a print of Freud's famous $33-million "Fat Lady" and dropped it in my lap. Famous as she may be, I had never seen "Fat Lady" before. Her name was "Big" Sue Tilly. Freud's portraits of "Big" Sue have long been the subject of much debate. Many saw the fat lady as repulsive and ugly. Some critics had even accused Freud of exploiting and objectifying her form. But I thought she was beautiful. Steadman explained that he had been looking for someone like me, like Freud's "Fat Lady," who would be willing to model for some time.

He described the scene he wanted with incredible detail: a bare me in repose on the blue futon and asked, finally, if I would be okay with posing nude. I would like to say that I thoughtfully and thoroughly considered the consequences of a nude painting and pictures of me floating around the universe and Internet forever, but that would be a lie. Seeing the painting of "Fat Lady" struck me—even though his audience saw "Fat Lady" as ugly, Freud had seen something that was worth seeing in the model. Steadman had seen something worth seeing. If someone else could see me as worthy, then I could, too. So I immediately said yes.

Before we started, he had one last question. How long did I think I could be still? To my eighteen-year-old self, just sitting around sounded easy enough. So I threw out a random number: forty-five minutes, an hour? Steadman wasn't impressed. Sitting for a painting was more than just sitting around. It was about embodying a feeling or idea. This required stillness of mind and body as well as control, not just passive sitting around. We settled on an hour. Feeling a little disheartened, I folded my clothes beneath the futon and took up my pose as Steadman directed.

Each arm, leg, knee, hand, and digit had to be just so. I had, of course, never considered the act of stillness in such depth before, but it presented an immediate challenge. Did I focus all my energy on the pose? Should I try to clear my mind and think of nothing? Or was I supposed to think of something specific so it showed in my expression? Steadman didn't have answers for any of these questions and said simply that it was different for everyone.

Steadman began to paint. Not knowing what else to do, I resolved to stare at one of the paintings hung on the opposite wall and wait until he said that I could move. The subject of the painting was a Bettie Page-esque burlesque dancer, a model friend of Steadman's. I studied her form for the entirety of that hour until it lost all discernible shape and bled into smears of color.

It flooded me with a familiar jealousy. She was beautiful and corseted thin. Just as I knew that my body was not worthy of being viewed, I knew what a worthy body looked like. The pretty dancer-model possessed all of the coveted traits that I knew I didn't have. What was more enviable than the model's pretty body was her obvious self-assurance. Her feet planted firmly in black stilettos, black hair tossed back, and a cool certain smile playing on her red lips. She was completely in control. It was impossible not to compare my body with hers, and I became extremely aware of my own form. Spread out before me, my body appeared horrible and vast. Each rise and fall of my chest and stomach in the cold air served as a reminder of my own largeness. To Steadman's annoyance, I began to fidget, grinding my teeth and digging my nails into my palms. But controlling my body also meant claiming ownership of it, and I didn't want mine. I wanted hers.

The envy mixed with guilt. Like all high school feminists, I had read bits of de Beauvoir, Steinem, and Plath. I knew women had long fought not to be re-rendered as objects and that was exactly what I had done, reduced the pretty burlesque dancer to nothing but envied shapes on canvas. Steadman had announced that I wouldn't be allowed to see the painting until it was finished. But I knew that even re-rendered I would never be looked at the way people must have looked at her. In that moment, it felt like an acceptance of defeat.

But I realize now that it was just an acceptance.

I spent six more days nude and supine on that blue futon. I came to care less and less about the final product and what it would look like. It became clear through the stillness and quiet of those six days that the ideas I had about myself and my physical worth were based on the way that I was seen through the lenses of other people. Even the way I saw myself was filtered through my short lifetime of conditioning on how I was expected to look. That load of expectations is far too heavy for anyone to bear. So I was able to let them go. It didn't mean that I immediately loved myself more or that I saw my body in a more flattering light.

But I decided then that the way I viewed my form and myself would no longer be determined by what other people saw.

Truce

Abby Weintraub

1) How badly do you want it?

"I can tell just by looking at you that you have PCOS. It stands for . . . "

"I know what it stands for," I interrupt quietly. Polycystic ovarian syndrome. It's almost comforting by now, the familiarity of these pronouncements. The well-worn territory of being told that all medical concerns are clearly related to the thing you can tell just by looking at me: that I'm fat.

"The thing is, I've been tested for it before, and . . ." I start, a tickle of frustration starting in my throat. *Don't cry, don't cry, don't cry.* I've been saying that to myself a lot lately. Every day, symptoms flood through my body like violent thunderstorms. Leaving bright clots like blobs of mercury on the sales floors at department stores as I run out, hoping nobody will notice until I'm gone. Knowing someone will have to clean up after me. Too ashamed to look back as I hail a cab I can't really afford, soaking the upholstery, desperate for home. *Don't cry.* There are no good solutions when you leave a trail of blood everywhere you go.

"It really doesn't matter," she stops me, waving a hand, leaning in, and lowering her voice conspiratorially. "Tests don't mean anything. Just lose the weight, and you'll be better. Seriously. I can't even tell you how many times I've seen this kind of thing, and the answer is always the same. It's just a matter of how badly you want to feel better." She sits back, her hands stretched out, as if generously presenting the answer I've been seeking my whole life. "It's up to you."

We stare at each other silently. *Don't cry. Don't fucking cry.* I consider tucking my tail between my blood-stained thighs, telling her I'll do my best. I consider announcing my medical rights, distributing fat liberation leaflets in the waiting room before bursting out onto 7th Avenue, alight with self-love and forward motion. Instead, I blink, shift and crackle in the gaping paper gown, look down, and bite my tongue hard as the hot tears start to come.

"Listen," she sighs, sitting on the metal stool and wheeling herself coolly to my side. Crossing one leg over the other, hooking the top foot behind the bottom calf, like the stripes of a candy cane. "I know it's hard. I know losing weight is easier said than done. I lost ten pounds a few years ago, and it . . . well, it sucked!" She chuckles gently, shaking her head at the memory of skipped desserts. "And I'm telling you: You can do it. Really, you can do anything you set your mind to."

I look up incredulously. Do I laugh at the flimsy pep talk or explain that I'm not crying because I want to lose weight? Or because "it's easier said than done"? Or because, as I fear she might think, her sympathy is so welcome and touching to me? I cry— the tears and snot sheeting down my cheeks now—because I *know* something is wrong. I know it in my bones, and nobody will help me, not this gynecologist, not others I've seen. Not the ER doctors who don't even bother to conceal their rolled eyes and shared glances when I'm wheeled in, half-covered in my own menstrual blood, sobbing from the pain, who send me home, doubled over and barely conscious, and tell me I'm fine.

With a blank, broken feeling settling over me, I nod, get dressed, and gather my things. "See you in a year!" she chirps behind me, but this is the last time I'll see any doctor for three years. And for those three years, I'll carry a malignant tumor around with me, tucked into a uterine wall. Growing slowly, left in peace to stretch its little fingers toward other plush, overlooked organs.

2] Before I continue

I don't want to spoil the ending, but just so you know, this won't be a story of "beating" anything. Not cancer, not fatphobia, not years of internalized self-hatred, not medical negligence, not the odds. This isn't the story of how I learned to be fabulous or fierce, nor how I fought a battle and emerged victorious or beaten. Much as I'd like there to be a narrative endpoint where my stories weave and seal together into a neat point, there isn't. The best I can do—and it's a full-time job even to do this—is attempt to balance medical rhetoric and prognosis with moral and political fury, self-love, confusion, failure, and the shame that sneaks up and humps my leg relentlessly. That's all. Are you still with me?

3] Citrus fruit and sporting equipment

The diagnosis started with easy concern and picked up enormous speed, like a penny dropped from a skyscraper, cracking the sidewalk below. I had needed a form filled out for grad school, and in the routine abdominal palpation, the doctor felt something. Probably fibroids, the doctor had said. Then there were MRIs, CT scans, urgent phone calls from the doctor. For two misdiagnosed weeks, before mine was pronounced an "easier" cancer, I curled into the numbness of a rare, largely untreatable disease. When not staring out of my Brooklyn window at the first snowfalls of the season, I tapped out Internet searches on my odds. Most likely, Google offered helpfully, I'd be dead within a year.

I had spent the previous three years with my body flying under the medical radar, hoping to avoid the "you're an undeserving drain on the health care system" looks. Meanwhile, the tumor had fattened itself to something between a grapefruit and a basketball; upon learning of its existence, I quickly developed an attachment to it. In those long stretches of shock-borne silence, I started to wonder why I should have more of a right to live than the cancer. Weren't we both just masses of organized cells driven by the urge to survive? To munch on our unsuspecting surroundings, growing ever larger and stronger? Hadn't the cancer and I stuck together through years of medical dismissal? For all the times that my symptoms were ignored and written off, the cancer and I were the only ones who'd known better. I felt protective of this confused tumor that had grown from my cells, every bit as much "me" as the organs in which it grew.

And despite so many people's best efforts, I never did find it in me to declare war. Not on the cancer, with all the military metaphors so often attached to it: attack, retreat, victory, battles lost and won. Not on my fat body, which I was told had made an especially hospitable nesting ground for the cancer. Not on the doctors who not only ignored the seriousness of my symptoms, but also blamed me for their existence to begin with.

Confronted with these options, I stared out the window and blinked for days, weeks, months.

4) The part I don't usually talk about

This is where I often stop telling the story. Or maybe I provide a few provocative details about the surgery, the treatment, the bed rest, the prognosis. But what I don't usually talk about is how, in the wake of my recovery, I started to lose weight. Ten pounds, twenty, fifty, a hundred. And though I sometimes feel I've gotten a kind of "get out of jail free" card from my fellow fat activists around the weight loss, I want to be clear about this: I did it on purpose. We're not supposed to talk about those choices, but I'm talking about them. I made changes to the way I ate and moved based on what I thought would best serve my physical comfort and chances of recurrence, and I lost a lot of weight. And I've gained a lot of weight since then, which is generally how it goes. I knew that would happen, and I did it anyway. My body—in size, health, self-acceptance—has never felt less static than in the years since my diagnosis. These changes are simple on my medical charts, and so, so complicated in my tender heart. Aren't they always, when it comes to our scrutinized bodies, and how they change over the course of a lifetime?

Recently, I've realized the similarity in language in people's reactions to the cancer and the weight loss: I had, in many people's view, beaten the odds. I had gone to war, in a battle so many have lost, and I emerged victorious. And suddenly, I was regarded as strong: so strong to have beaten cancer (as if my access to health care reflects a kind of inner strength; as if being split open, select organs removed, involved me in any kind of active, engaged way; as if the evil little cancer cells hijacked my otherwise pure and good body, which somehow dug in its heels and wrestled the bad guys to the ground). And in losing weight, I received even more praise around my "strength" than I did around surviving cancer (as if, again, I had won a battle so many spent their lives fighting; as if this was the end of a lifelong struggle, as opposed to just another point in the history of my body, which continues to change over time; and, of course, as if I would surely feel an enormous sense of relief at being smaller, now finally able to admit how weak I had been in my fatness).

More than anything, what I felt from other people's praise was a strong sense of their discomfort around bodies and an effort to find solid ground where there is none. We are ungrounded in the simple fact that bodies change, grow, shrink, and gain/lose ability over the course of a lifetime. We create a vocabulary of victors and defeat around bodies, trying to write heartwarming stories from cellular confusion. And where we create winners, there must be losers. If some are thought to have won battles with our own bodies, what of those who die with illness? Or those of us who are fat, whether in a gloriously self-loving way or in a way that wishes otherwise? Those of us who are disabled, chronically ill, depressed? It's tempting, when one is temporarily able, to imagine that such ability and "good health" are earned. Won. It's much more difficult to accept that our bodies are, by turns, miraculously high functioning and simply vulnerable.

5] Everything else

A story on the page is only a narrow slice of what happens. This one was the background (and sometimes foreground) music of my life for the last four years, but there's plenty more: I moved to the West Coast, fell in love once or twice, started a new job, got laid off, and so on. Following a brief I-survived-cancer-and-therefore-must-start-living-every-moment-to-the-fullest fervor, I settled back into the nest of everyday life. I'm just not wired for sustained, high-pitched urgency.

But not everything has gone back to normal. I remain unable to get behind any medical-, political-, or identity-based war that involves my body as target. I'm in menopause, which makes me hot and cold and irritable and calm and everything in between. It's changed the way I have sex, the way I communicate around my body with partners, the relationship I have to myself. I think about recurrence every day. My body continues to grow and shrink, and I work to accept the impermanence of its size, health status, and ability every day.

For now, I'm right here, in this body. Nice to meet you.

I Came to Femme through Fat and Black

Sydney Lewis

I came to Femme through Fat and Black; through freshly pressed hair sweat out in a dream about the girl with cherry lips and matching barrettes; through long brown Shirley Temple curls, white gloves, and look-up-her-skirt patent leather shoes during church services. The choir director gave me knowing winks. And, my pink dress was bought from Morrell's, a store for husky little girls who wanted to be beauty queens.

I came to Femme as sustenance through my first diet in the fifth grade. Where tuna fish and cottage cheese starved my 10-year-old body down from 167 to 135, still too Fat for my barely 5'0" frame, but thin enough for black stirrup pants, a green and yellow argyle sweater, and matching socks from The Gap. The sweater was just large enough to cover my womanly hips and rounded breasts, too shy for a bra. The Gap was just cool enough for my white friends to give me a pass into their sleepovers and pool parties, though fears of wet kinky hair and my baby fat booty kept my feet dangling in the shallow end.

I came to Femme for nurturing amidst my Mother's exclamations that she didn't know how something so big could have come out of *Her*. My mother is as beautiful as she is vain and didn't take kindly to the attention garnered by my already-luscious thighs peeking through the threads of my baggy cutoffs. Public humiliation was my punishment for "making" men older than my daddy lick their lips at me and whisper words I didn't understand. "Hussy" daggers bolted from her eyes, while admonishments about the nasty wants of men hissed through her clenched teeth. Twenty years later, Mother asks me why all her "light-skinned" children hate her, as if the distance between us is merely a matter of pigment and my feelings for her as uncomplicated as "hate."

I came to Femme for armor through middle school games of derisive dodge ball, where the ball hurled slurs like *Fat, Ugly, Nigger*, and *Faggot*, and I ducked and darted with good grades, trendy clothes, and year-long obsessions with white boys. Our dates were limited to the phone, which I cradled like a first love. While the boys bounced their balls for giggling blue eyes, I learned to keep my silence. After all, in dodge ball, Fat, Black girls are easy targets.

I came to Femme for esteem when my D-cups refused to fit primly into my size 14 eighth-grade dance dress—periwinkle flowers that matched with silver ballet flats. And when I realized that the pencils that the white boys dropped were specifically meant for me to bend over and pick up, I was humiliated . . . and flattered . . . and humiliated again. . . .

I came to Femme for dignity because I was not white, or blond, and certainly not petite. My nemesis, Heather, was all of these. I picked her orchid corsage to match her violet dress and offset her green eyes. Even in hatred, I still have impeccable taste. We had the same homecoming date, one week apart. I don't know who helped him pick out my corsage—probably his mom. It was a bruised white carnation. He was my first love. Heather was his.

I came to Femme laughing in red platform shoes, a tight sweater, and a lime green miniskirt—my campaign outfit to get my name on the prom queen ballot. I was an outcast among sun-bleached cheerleaders and skinny social-climbers. Some might call me the dark horse. But my life isn't a movie so I lost the big title and never got my *Carrie*-esque vengeance. A leftover ballot hangs on my bedroom wall, its frame decorated with flames and devil's horns—The Anti-Queen.

I came to Femme for a happy ending when I failed at slitting my wrists. In college, I camped in the library and combed fairy tales, looking for the stories that Disney forgot. In the real Cinderella, her ugly step-sisters cut off their toes in order to squeeze into the glass slipper. Understandable, I think, for a chance at happily-ever-after, or at least an end to being designated "The Ugly One."

I came to Femme in girl-drag practicing my supermodel strut, fierce in my tight red dress. RuPaul told me to "Werk!" my 235-pound body before blessing me with a kiss on the cheek. Drag queen kisses are like holy water, and Mother Ru baptized me.

I came to Femme for graduation after passing everything else, but failing assimilation. At 5'9" and 240 pounds, it is pretty hard to assimilate into anything. And when normalcy has been airbrushed, Femme gave me the makeup to be something else. Gold glitter glistens on my tan back Fat, and no one can wear teal eye shadow like a brown-eyed girl.

I came to Femme as defiance through a big booty that declined to be tucked under; through bountiful breasts that refused to hide; through insolent hair that can kink, and curl, and bead up, and lay straight all in one day; through my golden skin, against her caramel skin, against her chocolate skin, against her creamy skin; through rainbows of sweaters, dresses, and shoes; through my insubordinate body, defying subordination, incapable of assimilation, and tired, so tired of degradation; through flesh and curves and chafed thighs, which learned from my grandma how Johnson's Baby Powder can cure the chub rub; through Toni Morrison and Nella Larsen and Audre Lorde, and

Jewelle Gomez who, sometimes unwittingly, captured volumes of Black Femme lessons in their words; through Billie Holiday who wore white gardenias while battling her inner darkness; through my gay boyfriend who hummed show tunes and knew all the lyrics to "Baby Got Back," which he sang to me with genuine admiration; through shedding shame instead of shedding pounds; and through learning that growing comfortable in my skin means finding comfort in her brownness.

I came to Femme through FAT—where hunger becomes ravenous—and BLACK—where darkness meets danger. And with the click-clack of metallic heels and a not-so-little black dress, in Femme, I arrive.

Fat Histories, Fat Futures

Amithyst Fist & Genne Murphy

*A note from Amithyst and Genne: We met at the 2008
NOLOSE conference, the first that we had attended. The
National Organization of Lesbians of Size (NOLOSE)
hosts yearly or biyearly gatherings. An entire hotel is rented
out for the duration of a weekend. Fat-positive workshops
and plenaries are offered (on every subject from DIY fashion to erotica writing as a body love tool), meals are shared,
and fat community from all over the world is built.*

*In 2011, we decided to write a collaborative piece for
the Sunday Brunch Salon at that year's NOLOSE conference in Oakland, California. The theme for the salon was
"Fat Histories, Fat Futures." We thought it would be interesting to explore and contrast our fat pasts and the kind of
fat futures we saw for ourselves.*

*At the time, we lived on different coasts and saw each
other only at NOLOSE. We wrote the bulk of this piece via
phone and email over the course of a few weeks, finishing
it up in Amithyst's hotel room during the conference itself.*

It wasn't easy to write this, let alone read it in front of a conference of two hundred people. We were beyond nervous! But we were glad we did it. It was a defining and intense moment for both of us.

Below is our collaborative effort. We've made a few edits to prepare this as a written text, and also a few modifications that enabled us to feel more comfortable having this published—it's tricky writing about one's fat past, especially when referencing real people whom we love, who are a part of this past.

Fat Histories: Amithyst—Part 1

I was born in September, 1980, in San Jose, California, about forty miles from where we are right now in Oakland. I was born addicted to cocaine by parents who would now be considered hipsters. My mother was born in Italy but moved over to the new country when she was a small child. My father was born here in Oakland. When I was eight months old, my parents and I moved to San Francisco into a two-room flat in the Mission, on 24th and Guerrero; we lived in this flat until I was fourteen years old. Fifteen months after I was born, my mother gave birth to my brother. From our apartment, my mother cut hair, and my father was the biggest cocaine dealer in San Francisco in the 1980s. He sold cocaine to Robin Williams, David Crosby, Graham Nash, and a plethora of other burnt-out 1970s musicians and actors. Every night was a party at our apartment.

I remember pretending to be asleep and watching my parents snort thick lines off of Fleetwood Mac records. My favorite times were when my mother's drag queen friends used to come over; they would get high and dance around, and my mother would style their wigs. It all seemed so glamorous at the time.

Growing up, there were only three fat people in my life. Two were a distant dyke couple who used to be customers of my father. I was always so fascinated by them; I would sit on the dirty floor of the kitchen and just look up at them, mesmerized. Joyce, the butch, was strong and always wore A-shirts with her tattoos showing—she was midsized. Phyllis, the femme, was supersized, and always wore dresses and makeup. My mom would sometimes cut her hair, and I would always take pieces of her discarded hair and put it in my pillowcase.

I went to their house once because my father was making a delivery. They lived over the bridge in Marin County. Their house was modest with a huge rainbow flag blowing in the breeze of their front yard. They had lots of pet birds of all different colors and three dogs. We were only there for about fifteen minutes, but Phyllis let me play at her vanity with her makeup. I remember it feeling so right, and I knew that I wanted to be like her when I grew up. I knew that I was queer when I looked at Joyce and I *wanted* her (I mean as much as a six-year-old child can understand sexuality and wanting someone). But I knew that I wanted someone like *Joyce* versus someone like my father.

When I looked at Phyllis I saw strength—a different kind of strength than when I looked at her butch counterpart. I saw beauty that I had never seen before. I had never seen a woman that large before, never seen that much confidence and sex appeal from anyone. I was obsessed with them. I had daydreams of their adopting me, of their loving me and accepting me in ways my parents never did and never could.

The other fat person I knew was my Zia, my mother's sister. She was 5'0" tall and over three hundred pounds. I knew her weight at a very young age; my mother used to tell me at three years old, "Don't eat that or else you're going to be over three hundred pounds like your Zia." My Zia was the joke of the family, the embarrassment, the one everyone made fun of behind her back, the one everyone commented on about her food intake. No one seemed to pay attention to what anyone else ate . . . except for my Zia. Everyone knew how much she ate. I always felt sad for her.

When I started to get bigger, everyone began to comment on

what and how much *I* ate. My teenage cousin began making fat jokes about me at age six. I remember hiding in the pool shed crying while he made some joke about my belts being special-made out of ropes.

My mother had conflicting issues around food. A lot of Italians show love through food; it is just part of our culture. My mother probably hugged me five times in my whole life, but every time I visit her house she sends me home with Tupperware containers exploding with food and bags and bags of bulk food items. My mother can't hug me or tell me she loves me, but she will feed me and feed me . . . and then in the same second tell me how fat and disgusting I am.

Fat Histories: Genne——Part 1

The short story of my fat history is this: I was born. I grew up in a loving family. I became fat at age eight, which sucked. I lost weight as an older teen. I first entered fat community in my early twenties as an "in-betweenie," and I slowly found my way back to fatness in the years after, and to new understandings about bodies and identities, and loving myself and other people.

The end!

So, part of me would love it if that was the whole story and I could end here, and we could go back to Amithyst. As if I could wash my hands of any messy or painful realities of my history— or my present. I am ashamed by this desire of mine; it feels like running away. And because Amithyst has so eloquently opened her heart and her history to us, it would be wrong for me to run away, right?

I was born in Philadelphia in January of 1982 and raised in West Philly. I am close to my parents, two siblings, and extended Italian–American family. Similar to Amithyst, food was love in our household. Any meal was a celebration of food, family, and taste! Until my Grandmom Rita died, I couldn't leave her house without containers of soup, fresh eggs, cheese, vegetables, or fruit.

My mom cooks dinner while also planning and talking about breakfast at the same time and the wonderful leftovers she plans to give me for lunch. I'm also lucky that my family has been generous with physical affection and emotional support. My parents sought to give my siblings and me stability, structure, guidance, and a sense of the larger world, our place in it, and a responsibility to do right by other people.

As a fat kid, this base of love was the shelter I sometimes ran to when things got too hard, even if I wasn't always honest with my parents about what happened when I was out in the world. I really hated being a fat kid who was also shy, sensitive, and awkward. I desperately wished I was funny or charming or any of the things that might distract people from my fatness and notice that I was a good person, a loyal person, a dreamer, and a writer. I had an open face. My pop loved that he could read everything that was going on in my heart by looking at my face, but I didn't. This made me a natural target for bullies as a child, and later an easy mark for creepy men as I rode the trolley and subway home from school, men who cemented an early and negative connection between fat and sex for me.

I'm going to talk about bullies now, which feels like ripping a Band-Aid off or digging out a splinter. Actually it feels a lot worse than that to talk about, and maybe that's because my heart is still working out the shame, and I worry it will show on my face.

There were the teenage boys in my neighborhood who harassed me daily from age eight to age fourteen. They called me just one name, and it's something I've only said out loud once before in my adult life: Lard Ass.

The first time was to some trusted friends. We talked about how Lard Ass is strange sounding, worse than being called Fat Ass. Anyway, things got worse and worse with those boys; whole packs of them would follow me around and taunt me, throw sticks at me. One day two of them cornered me on my block and physically assaulted me. I was eleven. They roughed me up, groped me, and then found some piece of old, dirty tire and put it in my mouth. In hindsight, it could have been a lot worse, but I've never told any of my friends or partners about it because I don't like to think about how I didn't fight back. I thought I deserved to be beat up and ridiculed and made to feel dirty. My little sister was there, and I was so ashamed for her, that she had to see it, and hoped she wouldn't think less of me. She did tell my parents, and although the boys eventually got in trouble, I just felt more ashamed that my parents found out.

When I developed into a fat kid, my mother became a bit concerned. She earnestly encouraged me to think about my food intake and to exercise well into my teen and early adult years. She identified as a former chubby kid herself, and I think she wanted to protect me from those who would hurt me out in the world, or even those closer to home. For instance, one extended family member praised me for cleaning my plate as a young child, but when I got older would ask why I ate so much, point at my ripples of belly fat, and tell me they were shelves that she could put things on. I did go on to lose weight in high school and college, not through dieting, per se (although I did skip meals here and there) but through years of intense exercise. I was an athlete and enjoyed moving around, and activity did make me feel physically good and happy. But I had a hard time sorting out the healthy behaviors from the unhealthy ones. Let me be clear: I don't think there was anything wrong with my body when it was smaller. It was still mine. I still laughed and played and loved and cried in that body. What was wrong was the sense of safety I felt, the relief at being no larger than a size 12 or 14. What did I think I was safe from, exactly? The world? Fat haters? The memory of my former self?

First NOLOSE and Beyond: Amithyst—Part 2

I came out of the closet at thirteen years old. I felt supported by my parents when I came out as a lesbian. My parents accepted the fact that I was queer way more than they did or do accept my fatness. I struggled a lot in my young, fat, femme body, feeling like I had no place in the queer Mecca of early-1990s Portland. I would go to this gay underage nightclub every weekend, and I was the only fat person there *ever*. I would look at all the other young dyke couples and feel so out of place, like I would never fit in. I felt lost and confused and like a minority within the minority. When I was fourteen, one of my friends invited me to see Bikini Kill at La Luna. It was at this show that I learned about the riot grrrl movement. I met other fat, queer kids at this show when I was outside smoking pot. It was like I had found my home, which I had been searching for in the mainstream gay and lesbian underage club. I dived head first into riot grrrl, reading every zine I could get my hands on about body image issues and fat positivity. I started to love myself more and more.

I first heard about NOLOSE in a LiveJournal community around 2002, and I knew that I had to attend. I first attended NOLOSE in 2008 when I was finally in a place in my life where I could afford to go across the country to attend a conference. NOLOSE changed my life; it gave me a sense of safety and community I had never felt before.

At that year's conference, I attended a workshop that Genne did about "intergenerational fat voices." She had interviewed her grandmother about her experiences growing up as a fat woman and Italian–American in a small, white, working-class American town in the 1930s, '40s, and '50s. I had never met Genne before, but in the description she talked about her Italian heritage and being queer and fat. I had been craving connection (and still do) with other queer Italians. So I knew I had no choice but to attend, and I am so glad I did. Genne prompted us to write about the intersection of family and fatness. Genne got me thinking about my family and started me on my way to actually having conversations with my family about my choices regarding my body. Due to drug addiction and other factors, my parents moved me to Portland as a teen. In Portland, there is no Italian community like I had during the first half of my life in San Francisco. I get really excited any time I meet another Italian person, and another queer Italian person sends me right over the edge with excitement. This workshop was so intimate, and there was so much love expressed in the conversations between Genne and her grandmother. I felt almost an instant connection with Genne. While we have a lot of differences in our lives, we also have a lot of similarities. NOLOSE gives us a space to create these magical connections even though we only see each other once a year.

First NOLOSE and Beyond: Genne—Part 2

In my early twenties, I began thinking about what my future body might look like. I'd visit my beloved Grandmom Rita, who had struggled with her weight for most of her life and think: this will be me one day. I'd look at old black-and-white photos of her and notice the parallels: same smile, same variations in size at specific ages. Yet being like her didn't seem like a horrible fate. Rita was, after all, gorgeous and generous and kind. Entering her kitchen was like coming home. She cooked in an easy and informal way, tasting and smelling and loosening her curled up, arthritic hands while she kneaded dough or rolled meatballs. She sometimes ignored recipes and just worked on a dish until it "looked just right." She liked that phrase—the people she loved, to her, we "looked just right," too. I'd walk into her kitchen and she'd say: "Genne, you're so beautiful, inside and out, I'm so lucky to be around you" like five or six times, and she'd smile and touch my face. I don't think I've ever known anyone, ever, who so genuinely and thoroughly proclaimed my beauty, every time they saw me, no matter my size, or the clothing I wore, or the way I presented myself.

One day at a party, I met someone who eventually became one of my best friends, and a first fat femme mentor—Zoe. The first time I saw her from across the room I thought: "Wow, she's drop-dead gorgeous." We talked and eventually began hanging out and cooking together. We'd make delicious pastas and sauces and other

Italian dishes, our basic comfort foods growing up. Zoe celebrated meals and food like my extended Italian family did, but minus the occasional conversations about Weight Watchers. The more I got to know her, the more she reminded me of some of the strong, brilliant women in my family. Zoe was the kind of person I strived to be: kind and smart and thoughtful and fierce as hell. I credit Zoe as one of the first people who helped me to politicize fatness and introduced me to radical fat community. I'd hang out with Zoe and think, "Oh. I get it now. I get how it could be." But she was also a sounding board for many conversations about the personal, complex, and sometimes painful relationship of fat and family.

Before my first NOLOSE in 2008, I got permission from my grandmother to interview her about her experiences around fatness to present in a workshop. She was intrigued by my description of NOLOSE, but didn't ask too many questions. In my own way, I saw this as an opportunity to bring Rita with me to this space—a space I knew she was never going to see for herself. She blew me away with the history she shared—her father who called her a fat cow and "mooed" at her as a child and early teen; the fact that she never learned to dance because no boys ever asked her; the doctor who put her on a diet while she was pregnant; the years she never ate cake or milkshakes before finally starting to do so in her seventies because even if she still disliked parts of her body she hated the dieting more. I realized more clearly why Grandmom Rita never seemed to recognize in herself the beauty she saw in me: in Rita's own eyes she was sometimes ugly and stupid and she could never do anything right.

When Amithyst sent me an early draft of her part of this writing, I found out for the first time how meaningful that workshop was to her and how this led to conversations with her own family about food and fatness. I then listened to the interviews with Rita for the first time since 2008. I cried through most of it because she had died in March 2012 and I missed the sound of her voice, but I also thought a lot about all the ways her fat history twined and curled into my mother's and later mine and how sharing that history eventually affected Amithyst. It made me think about all the ways we can layer upon each other's fat histories and learn from one another and hopefully figure out better futures together.

Fat Futures: Amithyst—Part 3

NOLOSE gives me a venue to have difficult conversations and to reach out and seek support around my personal demons. Like most of us, I have plenty of demons that I am working through by choice or by force.

In my parents' footsteps, I struggle with my own addictions, and I have overcome a lot of them through rehab programs and counselors. I have overcome a heroin addiction, a meth addiction, and an addiction to abusive partners. I still struggle with a smoking habit and a very serious food addiction.

I have a very hard time talking about my food addiction. While I've been fat most of my life, my food addiction definitely plays into the size of my body and maybe even vice-versa. Much like my mother, I equate food with love. When I feel rejected, food is my love. When I feel alone, I go to food. When I want to be okay with myself, I turn to food. When I need to escape from my body because I can't deal with all the PTSD and pain and I need a break from living in this world as a supersized person, I turn to food. I am struggling daily to love myself, to love my super-fat body, and to take care of my body in a way that doesn't have to mean losing weight.

For the past two years, my body has begun to show signs of what my mother has always said would happen. My lower back and knees hurt a lot. Going up stairs pretty much kills my knees, ankles, and back. Walking more than two blocks also has this effect on my body. My mother was right about what she's been telling me for years: that things would catch up with me as I age. I have been trying to be present in accepting these facts and trying to be proactive about them. I have begun to try to live in my body for the first time in thirty years, trying not to disassociate, and trying to let myself feel my weight and the pain in my body.

I have been attending a "Yoga for Fat Bodies" class. I was really scared to attend the first time, but after the class, and the next day, I felt so much less pain in my body. I have been going to get acupuncture anytime I have an extra $30. Acupuncture has helped with the swelling in my ankles and the pain in my knees—there is some magic that happens with acupuncture. I am trying the best that I can in my messy life to heal myself of my eating disorder and to love myself, truly LOVE MYSELF.

Fat Futures: Genne—Part 3

I wish I could shake off every morsel of shame about this body of mine and its journey *right now*. But I guess this takes years to unlearn, and there's always something new to figure out. I've ultimately been grateful to talk through many things with Amithyst. We saw this as an opportunity not only to learn a little more about one another, but also to try to stumble through and unpack things together. The other night we were talking about how nervous we were, and how long we thought our piece is, but how we haven't really scratched the surface. Amithyst said she was a little scared to share her feelings about food, food addiction, and getting older, but then said: "I feel like I have to. And NOLOSE is the safest and scariest place to do it."

I'm eternally grateful that being fat and radical has allowed me to get fatter as an adult without the shame I'd probably feel otherwise and to be way more confident than I ever was. Although my parents struggled financially the first part of my childhood, they eventually reached middle class and were able to provide me a stable and comfortable home and an education. The privilege of being white and middle class, for me, cushions some of the things that are challenging about being fat and queer and a woman, just as my current size and shape afford me privilege within this community and the greater world. Plus, the luck of being born into a family that loved me well, it's only in the last few years that I've realized that my Grandmom Rita telling me "you're beautiful" every chance she could get was a gift. I think if she'd known Amithyst throughout her life she would have told her the same, that she is obviously so beautiful and so lovely and smart and kind. But because she's not here to say it, I'll take the gift she gave me, and pass it along: "You're beautiful and lovely and just right."

I've been upset reading parts of Amithyst's story. Our lives converge in interesting ways—our families' relationship to food, our parents' support of our queer lives and discomfort with our fat lives, and our similar experiences with loved ones who are addicts or users. But then there are things that are so different about us: our fat pasts and our fat futures. Amithyst came to fat community as a supersized person, and I came to fat community when I was at my smallest size without an easily recognizable fat past. When we look ahead at our thirties and beyond, there is a gap between us in what we expect our bodies to be able to do and how we think the world will interact with us. But here we are, sitting together, and I am glad that NOLOSE provided two fat queers like us, from different coasts, with individual stories, to meet and laugh and cry and work some shit out together.

I recently wrote a piece with my father about family and what it means to us. I feel blessed by all the love in my life, and for me, "chosen family" encompasses my various queer and fat communities and many members of the family I was born into, including my awesome parents and siblings. In writing with my father, I realized that it is the act of choosing that is most important; this choosing of one another, every day, that makes a family.

I'd like to extend that to our fat community, which is amazing and sometimes hard and always changing: it is the act of choosing one another every day that makes this a community worth building together. Choosing to listen and learn from one another, even when it's hard, and to hold one another accountable for making space here—and in the greater world—that encompasses our range of histories, experiences, and current realities. It's up to us to choose how to dream a future together and then to make it happen.

Our Goals for Our Fat Futures: Amithyst

My goal for my fat future is to unlearn to use food as love; to use love as love; to not be scared to tell people when I'm scared, hurt, lonely, or struggling; to be able to talk about my knees/back hurting and feeling like my body is falling apart; to talk about getting older without shame and about fears of getting older and fatter honestly; and to reach out to folks when doctors tell me that if I don't have gastric bypass surgery I will die, when we all know that quite the opposite is true.

My goal is to keep coming to NOLOSE to be able to connect to other supersized folks and to talk about how amazing and hard it is to be at NOLOSE as a supersized person. It's fucking beautiful, but it's also really hard to be the fattest of the fat.

My goal is to love myself and my fat queer community immensely and to support each other and fight together like our lives depend on it because they really fucking do.

Our Goals for Our Fat Futures: Genne

To find more ways to take the good things I learn from the people at NOLOSE and bring it back into my everyday life and my relationships outside of the fat community.

To learn how to let go of the hard stuff and let the good stuff in. To let my heart show on my face like it did when I was a kid.

To be the best ally I can be to other fat people, to listen, to figure out what your story is, and to let you tell it.

Hey Sisters, Welcome to My World

Charlotte Cooper

I've been into fat for a long time. We're talking decades. The moments of awakening into fat identity have long passed for me. Fat is now something that is deeply embedded; it's at the heart of my creative, social, sexual, political, and professional lives. Today was a really quiet day. I worked on my thesis, wrote a blog post, wrote this, talked to a couple of people—all of this was all about fat. I did some gardening, walked to the shop, ate avocado on toast, witnessed someone talking about diets. I daydreamed about fat. Fat's there in pretty much everything, the dull as well as the thrilling stuff, do you know what I mean?

At this stage in the game, it feels cheesy and restrictive to talk about my experiences of being fat as positive or of myself as a fierce fatty. I balk when people lecture me about loving my body. Perky was never my scene. One of the things I love about fat is the way you can use it as a lens, the way it changes things and enables you to understand them differently, like when I saw a chubby young girl dancing with her friends on a fairground ride in Vienna's *Wurstelprater* I didn't regard her as a tragic victim of the Global Obesity Epidemic™ which, perhaps, is what I was supposed to have seen. Instead I wondered how she came to dance so freely. The joy is there in the understanding. I'm not denying that peeping through the lens does not have to be about becoming conscious of unrelenting grimness. I listened to a recording of a radio show made by fat activists in Boston in the early 1980s the other day; that was a pleasure and a half. I suppose I just want to say this: fat for me is very complicated—in a good way. It's part of how I see things.

When I think of my fat activism, I think of it as a project of disruption. One of my favorite fat people is Brigid Polk, also known as Brigid Berlin. Brigid is a poor little rich girl who joined the party at Andy Warhol's Factory in New York in the 1960s and never left. A once-raging speed-freak, Brigid is a woman with what looks to me like a tenuous grip on reality, a sufferer of a lifelong eating disorder, a representative of reprehensible privilege, a maker of far-out art. Brigid is a messy kind of person, self-hating in many ways. She's not straightforwardly loveable; she's no puppy. You could hardly call her a fat-positive role model. In photographs of the Factory crowd, she's always at the margins, usually naked or with a breast flopping out of her top accidentally on purpose, glowering, probably on drugs, far fatter than anybody else in the frame. Blurp, she's there and you can't look away, you can't deny her; she won't be cut out of the picture. I love her because, like the wicked witch gate-crashing the fairy princess's christening, her presence undermines the beautiful people in the picture and the stupid values they embody. That's what makes her the one to watch. I think of those photographs often; they really inspire me. Brigid's insolence is so beautifully, deeply punk.

Earlier this year, I had the opportunity to cause a bit of trouble myself. I submitted a proposal for a workshop and got invited to present the plenary session at an academic conference in the North of England. I know this sounds like the dullest thing on earth and is not an auspicious start to the story. Please bear with me. The conference was devoted to feminist cultural activism. I wanted to talk about my girl gang, The Chubsters.

I started The Chubsters in 2003 after watching Katrina del Mar's low-budget short film *Gang Girls 2000* and wishing there was more flesh on screen. It started off as a joke for a magazine photo-story and has been morphing and mutating since. I think of The Chubsters as a platform for different kinds of fat activism. It's a fat queer girl gang, but you don't have to be fat, queer, a girl, or remotely tough to be a part of it. There are real-life and imaginary elements to it. There are card-carrying members who have been jumped-in, whatever membership means. The gang uses symbols and ideas; it's a kind of fantasy that leaks out into the real world from time to time through workshops and objects. In a context where fat activism often has very definite parameters, The Chubsters is an anomaly; it disrupts ideas of how things should be. There's no constitution, no regular meetings, no membership roll call, no fixed position; who can be bothered with that stuff? It's so boring! Sometimes this makes people (i.e., academics who want to appropriate this newfangled thing called "fat activism") very uncomfortable which, of course, I enjoy.

I began the session by trying to explain what The Chubsters is about. I said that the gang is rooted in fat activism, DIY culture, punk, prankishness, queer and trans community, as well as revolutionary rhetoric. I described the gang as a project that creates an idealized universe where fat people have power, where freakhood is capital, and where nobody messes with us. The Chubsters heartily endorse the pleasures of refusing to be nice and ladylike. It's a project that emphasizes antisocial behavior rather than pleading assimilation, asserting moral correctitude, or respecting rational argument. There you go, now you know.

I hate it when people make me do stuff in a workshop and even more so when they make people divide into groups to do an activity or have a discussion. Just leave me be! Don't push me around! Folks were able to leave if they wanted to, but The Chubsters is not a democracy. The people who stayed were going to have to do things my way, and this entailed getting into small groups. I reasoned that a big room full of feminist academics interested in feminist activism would be well into skill-sharing; it sounds so right-on and egalitarian, right up their street. So I decided that we would use the session to skill-share some killer Chubster moves:

- **Glaring:** The first group was invited to perfect their most hostile facial expression.
- **Shooting:** I drew targets of Slim-Fast cans, handed out potato guns (metal toys that shoot pellets of potato), and encouraged the second group to aim and fire.
- **Spitting:** I drew a BMI chart, symbol of fat people's oppression, and called upon the third plenary group to spit on it with flamboyance and style.
- **Freestyle:** This was a free space for people who didn't want to glare, shoot, or spit, but who would be encouraged to fight dirty by any means necessary.

Some of the happiest moments of my life have been when I have successfully goaded a large number of people into doing something completely stupid and bizarre for my own amusement. So this is what power feels like! Nice! I remember once telling off some kids for misbehaving in a queue for a theme-park ride and being really surprised that they did what I asked them to do. I had fully expected them to shove their ice creams in my face and run off laughing, "So long, sucker!" I was now having flashbacks to that incident. I couldn't believe that I had so much authority and that the people in the room were doing exactly as they were told.

In their ordinary lives, the plenary participants are professors, graduate students, and good, right-thinking, upstanding, liberal citizens. A pie chart of their reading habits would probably reveal a large slice devoted to *The Guardian*. The participants were wearers of fleece and sensible shoes; by and large, white middle-class women were well-represented. Few were fat like I am fat. The workshop temporarily transformed them.

The glaring group had soon formed a quiet circle in the lecture theater where the session was being held and were busy giving each other the most evil and aggressive looks, sometimes accompanied by a pointing finger. You really would not want to mess with these people.

Across the way were the freestylers who had decided to arm-wrestle each other. When I came back to warn them that the session would soon be ending, I found them physically attacking each other on the lecture theater carpet, wrestling and wrasslin', no holds barred, a blur of hair and arms waving around, the group cheering each other on.

Outside, on a little grassy hill, no doubt usually reserved for earnest theoretical discussions over sandwiches and tea, the shooters were going ape for the spud guns, shooting every which way like Annie Oakley. Those Slim-Fast cans did not stand a chance.

I stayed with the spitters. I have wanted to spit accurately and with nonchalant ease for many years, ever since I saw Patti Smith shoot a jet of gob out of her mouth to the side of the stage one time, and now was my chance to learn. To cajole a group of nice people into spitting seemed particularly daring; to spit is pretty disgusting. There are cultural ramifications to spitting, especially women spitting. It is really not nice. I shouldn't have worried; the spitters did not let me down. We stood together in a little huddle and spat until we'd run out of juice. We spat on the move, running past the target, from a great distance, spitting close up, spitting fast, spitting slow, and hawking up a big greenie and depositing it with a precise and satisfactory finesse. We attempted backward spitting, quick-draw spitting, one limber woman bent over into a crab and—PTOO!— let go a graceful arc of spittle that landed smack dab in the middle of the target. Here's a secret: Spitting is a lot of fun.

What I remember most is the delight, the laughter, and the mischievous sparkling eyes that I saw amongst the people participating in this wild session. People were over-tired from the conference and needed to let off steam, which I was only too happy to facilitate. I often feel deeply alienated from the academy, but this feral space felt very much like home. There weren't many fat people in the crowd, but it was as though I'd given everyone the opportunity to experience the best of what it feels like to be fat: free, together, badass, profoundly embodied, gorgeously gross, full of joy and possibility and life, completely lacking in tragedy, abjection, pity. Hey sisters, welcome to my world.

Coda: After the session was over and it was time to pack up, someone helped me dispose of the revolting spit-covered BMI chart. No way was I taking this home. The pair of us heaved a little as we wrangled it to the bin, trying to avoid the gobs of phlegm that were dripping off it. There's an image of a spit-covered BMI chart that now lives in my subconscious, an image that perfectly represents my view of BMI and all it stands for. Maybe other people will remember this image, too. I am not alone with it; we made this image possible together. I imagined it and helped it exist in real life. I'll call on this image whenever I need it. It will give me strength when I am vulnerable. It already makes me cackle.

I'll never forget it.

Big Yoga Student

Kimberly Dark

She was checking me out. No, really, you can feel that sort of thing, right? Her gaze lingered as I walked into the yoga studio—just that split second longer than a usual acknowledgement. She caught my eye as I rolled out my mat. She looked me up and down—quickly, not in a creepy way—and smiled broadly. Then, as I was picking up a blanket and a block, I could feel her eyes follow me.

So, was there some kind of come-on coming on? A budding yoga studio romance to ensue? I can tell you from experience that this glance likely had a different origin than erotic *tapas*.

We're fat women in a fitness setting.

I know the look—have experienced it for more than twenty years now at yoga studios, gyms, and aerobics classes. I'm accustomed to being looked at because I'm surprising—shocking even. I'm a large woman, and dare I say it—relatively fit, despite being more than one hundred pounds overweight by insurance chart standards. The woman who stared and smiled? She's fit and fat, too. And if she hadn't been so openly interested in looking at my body,

I'd have been sneaking peeks at hers, catching glimpses of how her thighs appear in those stretch pants and how her belly or arm fat protrudes from her spandex tank top. The looking is better than the not looking. Sometimes a fat woman will avert her gaze from my flagrant display of largesse. But we were both at peace, happy to see each other. I can't guess what my admirer was thinking, but based on her smile, I will consider her kindred. Perhaps we were having the same thought: "How wonderful! She's living her life and using her body as she chooses, despite what others might think."

Part of why we find solidarity with one another is because we're scarce—at least at swank studios like that one. When I first started practicing yoga, twenty years ago, there was a range of bodies moving—sometimes struggling—through the postures. Yoga moves seemed a little eccentric and only the bold among us took them into daily life. Back then, I'd catch stares when practicing at the airport in hopes of finding some back-ease mid-flight. You know, those kind of "don't look now, but there's a fat woman doing freaky stuff just over your left shoulder" stares. Sometimes I'm so out-of-the-norm it's hard to tell which aspect of me is being gawked at. However, I receive some glances so frequently, I could make a study.

Nowadays it's easy to recognize the yoga-faithful in public places: the eagle arms in the park at noon on a Tuesday, a deliberate uttanasana at Gate 23, the Virabadrasana I on the beach. Yoga has expanded its reach, but in the process, it's left some of us behind. The great adjustments, clear instructions, and careful attention to detail of the better yoga studios come with a daunting environment of fitness fanaticism. It's no mystery why these studios market to the fitness faithful. They pay. And the rest of us just don't fit in.

Yes, yes, we're practicing *yoga*, so we should all just go within and release our self-judgments. Whoa now. We're working on that, but some have a steeper climb. Or do we? Perhaps it's just easier to look comfortable when one's ego attachment is to the perfect titibasana and the $100 recycled yak fur yoga mat. It's inevitable in a consumer culture that the people who can afford to pay a yoga teacher what she's worth will be interested in status. And "hot body" in America definitely equates status. Sometimes the noble fat person can sneak through—the beginner who's assumed to be fighting the good fight against her or his own flab. That person can be jovially accommodated and feel a little bit of love. But what of the average plodder who does a regular practice and never "looks" fit? Well, sometimes it's just not comfortable, so the group support and individual instruction offered by beautiful studios are forfeit.

And that's part of why I became a yoga teacher. Let me not sound too noble here—I love teaching; I've taught a lot of things in a variety of ways for years. And teaching deepens my practice. In addition to these common motivations, I also have a desire to model difference—to encourage others to live fuller lives and to love themselves with greater ease. And sometimes this is personally challenging in ways that it isn't for someone who looks the part, though surely personal doubts about credibility can assail anyone. I've had students at more fitness-oriented establishments see me, look aghast, and walk right out of the class. I've also subbed for classes where students see me and ask if it's going to be a "gentle" class today. To which I jovially respond, "Oh no! We're really gonna kick some ass!"

Ten years ago, I would make the effort to prove my fitness worthiness, but nowadays, I just make my own offering, flawed and brilliant as it can be. (And for pity's sake, if you can't focus on your own breath and asana through a 90-minute class that isn't what you thought you wanted, keep practicing baby. Just keep practicing.)

We need more fat yoga teachers and old yoga teachers and disabled yoga teachers and anyone with a different body than you think you want. That's what this mess is about, right? Most students want to think of the teacher's body as a goal, an attainable one because she got to look like that by doing this yoga thing. Well, it's not that simple, despite our desire to just pay, participate, and make it so. We want to hop on the yoga conveyor belt and plop off the end looking rested, flexing hot buns and deserving a martini (or a piece of chocolate cake—choose your poison). The bad news—and the good news—is that living a good life is more about acceptance than it is about attainment. Sure, change is possible, but it's not always the change you were taught to believe you should want.

So, are you thinking about going to a yoga class, but afraid you won't fit in? Chances are you don't. And go anyway. You and everyone else in the room will be better for it. And if you have a body that gets stares—and not always in a good way—and you want to teach, I encourage you. It really will deepen your experience to be the one demonstrating the beauty of a regular practice. Just remember, you may as well get up in front of the class to teach, they're looking at you anyway.

Like a Tiara

Laura Spafford

Let's start this thing out right. I'm fat. It's only until *very* recently that I have felt comfortable saying that out loud without being self-deprecating. I was always the big girl in class or the chunky one in the group. Even when I was thin, I was fat because my thin was always a little fatter than the other girls surrounding me. This was my plague. This was my constant battle. How was it that I was 5'2", 130 pounds, dancing twenty-five hours a week, wearing a size 6, and yet was still the fat girl? That is the life of a performer in a San Diego arts high school. I first became really body conscious in sixth grade because it was the first time I got treated differently for my size. I got put in the long-sleeved costume and the bathing suit with the skirt, put at the bottom of the pyramid, literally, in a dance.

I had many coping mechanisms in middle school and high school to maintain control of my body. I was a constant dieter, never ate in public, and drank so much water I probably had a vitamin deficiency just to fill the empty void I constantly felt in my stomach. Some days I'd eat nothing but saltines and dried apple rings. It was a struggle, and my body kept trying to betray me, but

I managed to stay under 145 pounds and never got above a size 8 through high school, yet I was still the heavy girl. I got good roles because I could sing, but it was tricky finding costumes that would fit because I was curvier than the costumers were used to. I was an inconvenience for them. I always dreaded the costume fittings after getting cast in a role because I had to go through the misery of the measuring tape. I'd hear exasperated exhalations from the dear women who were going to have to struggle to find something to cover my body. I was apologetic. I made excuses for my chub and promises to drop the weight before opening night. I never did, of course, but with a little extra effort on the part of the costumer I also never went on stage naked.

Under ordinary circumstances, I was a very normal-size girl and was pretty much always thinner than my sisters and mom. I thought I was fat, and appeared to be fat, because my thighs always touched. That's because they were muscular and my body is situated so as not to allow there to be a space between my thighs, no matter how slender they are. Also, my belly has always curved and pouched out a bit above my pubic bone. And I've always had cellulite and some extra meat on my hips since I started puberty. We're talking nine years old. Something in my genetics decided my body was meant to be soft and plump and dimpled. I tried everything I could to slim down and not eating helped for a while, but my hunger always won out in the end. I guess I just wanted my body to look like the other naturally slender girls, so I tried to force it into a mold. It did not cooperate.

I was lucky to attend a performing arts high school and get a chance to do what I loved every day. Many of my directors went out on a limb with me, casting me in leading lady roles over older, thinner, and more experienced classmates. As I got older and my body continued to develop more womanly curves and softness, in spite of my constant struggle to suppress it, the roles I played became more womanly and curvaceous. Are a 36" hip, 28" waist, and a B-cup really "curvy"? It seemed to be, so I eased up a little and tried to enjoy my body. It was hard to come to terms with the fact that I wasn't going to look like the rest of the girls I was competing with. Scandinavian heritage had blessed me with thick, blond hair, clear blue eyes, and fair skin. It also made me built like a milkmaid: sturdy, solid, with child-bearing hips. I made do with what I had and was successful in high school. I made a name for myself in my little community.

Then I went to college. I dealt with stress I was unfamiliar with. I had more competition than I was used to and teachers who didn't know me. They saw just another pretty, chubby girl who needed to drop some weight to be considered. I was, as a musical theater major, still dancing close to twenty hours a week, taking yoga, teaching dance on the side, and walking more than a mile round-trip to get from my dorm to campus several times a day. I was also eating on a college student budget, cooking for myself for the first time, and going to parties, and my body was still developing. I am just not supposed to be a skinny girl. I was under a lot of scrutiny and for the first time dealt with rejection. I was a chubby octopus in an ocean full of talented, skinny fish, and for once, I was passed over for roles because I was lacking a look. When I "ballooned" up to 155 pounds, I was horrified. How could I be a size 10? How could I let myself get bigger than my clothes? How could I be this fat when I exercise so much? So, after two years of school, trying to make a long-term relationship work, and a lot of homesickness, I gave up and moved home, heavy hearted and heavy bodied.

After the big breakup with Boyfriend #1, who after four years left me for a girl whom I viewed as a thinner, prettier version of me, my weight dropped back to 140 pounds. It happened mostly because I was depressed and terrified of all the changes I was going through. I wasn't performing anymore except for the occasional chorus role. I started replacing theater with men. Being single for the first time in four years, I was scared that no one would have sex with me if I was fat. Looking back on that now, I see how concerning that was. I wasn't worried about school. I wasn't worried about getting my life on track. I wasn't at all worried about finding love. I knew someone would love me someday because I'm awesome. I knew that at some point in my life, regardless of my size, love would come to me. It's amazing looking back now to think that I had that subconscious awareness. I wish I would have listened a little more seriously to it, but at twenty years old, after a devastating heartbreak, I wasn't looking for love anymore. I just wanted someone to have sex with me, and if it was going to be purely physical, I would need to be thin. Because thin = fuckable. Right? Right?!? If only I could have had some of the confidence I had in my personality and directed it toward my body.

I tried to fit into the party-girl mold when I turned twenty-one. I was doing small roles in community theater productions and leaving the theater after performances to go to bars so boys there would flirt with me, buy me drinks, and sometimes make out with me in an ally while sharing a cigarette. I used a good amount of these men for sex. It was empowering. I really wasn't getting the big roles I was used to and missed the applause. So I looked for approval somewhere other than a casting director because, clearly, that wasn't working out. By this time in my life, my weight was steadily increasing and I was okay with that because men had astounded me with positive feedback. As far as I was concerned, if men found me interesting, charming, attractive, and still wanted to sleep with me even if my belly and thighs were round and squishy, I was okay with that. As long as I was getting male validation, I was going to be okay.

I was creeping past a size 12, tiptoeing into the plus-size departments, and learning about the wonders of having real breasts and hips and how I could use those things to my advantage. Cleavage can get you anything from free drinks to theater tickets, but it doesn't always get you parts. I stopped auditioning, stopped dancing, and got a desk job. I also dated a lot, and in these relationships, which came one right after the other, I got fat. I got E-cup, size

18 jeans, XXL top, walk-right-past-Charlotte-Russe-because-Lord-knows-nothing-will-cover-your-ass fat. I was 215 pounds at 5'2". My feet got too fat for my shoes. I had to go get good bras because for once I actually had something to lift. I weighed more than my sister when she was full term in her pregnancy. I'd pushed performing to the background, started working full time, and tried to cope with the demise of my waistline. I was still trying to convince myself that I was supposed to be a fit, trim, slender girl. I thought I had just let myself get fat and I just needed to buckle down and lose the weight. If I did that, then maybe I could get on track with my life. Land a good role. Get back to school. Find joy in being a performer again.

Then I met a woman named Margitte. She was one of the most beautiful women I had ever seen. She's also the first person I had ever heard use the term *fat activist*. She was the first person I had ever heard speak honestly about fat: the word, the stigma, the fact that it was something I didn't need to be ashamed of. She was a fabulous, sassy, smart, well-spoken, gorgeous fat woman, and I realized I wanted to emulate her. I didn't need to be afraid of what my body had turned out to be. I started reading her blog (http://www.RiotsNotDiets.com), as well as a lot of other fat-positive blogs and learned about the Health at Every Size Movement. I realized that I didn't have to be ashamed of my body. I learned that I can be perfectly happy and healthy and lead a fulfilling life regardless of my shape and size and not be ashamed of my fat. I'm not ashamed or afraid of the word *fat* or what it means to be labeled as such anymore. I've taken that title, and I'm wearing it like a badge of honor.

Like a tiara.

I wear fat like silk stockings on smooth skin. It's a beautiful thing. And I started performing again! I decided that I love to perform way too much to just give up on it because I didn't fit into the character mold I thought was right for me. So I started auditioning again! I was in a swing music review in the summer of 2011 and was cast in the vocal ensemble. During the first rehearsal, I looked at the other ladies I was going to be performing with and I realized that I was by far the largest person in the cast, male and female alike. I was flanked by wonderful, beautiful, kind, and *very* slender people. But I picked up the music and choreography just as easily as they did. Costuming was a bit of a challenge as the idea was that we would all wear floor-length beaded gowns in gold or black. The costumer had to special order my dress because floor-length vintage beaded gowns don't exist in a size 18, so we went with a black chiffon sheath. It was a size XXL and we found it online and the costumer put the gold piping on the empire waist. I saw some pictures from the show recently and there I was, in the middle, my big, soft arms with charming dimples at the elbow out for the world to see and prominent double chin casting shadows on my cleavage. I wish I wasn't wearing black so you could see a better outline of my body, especially in comparison to the lovely golden girls on either side. I stuck out like a sore thumb a bit, but luckily my director wasn't one to get caught up in body-image bullshit and was happy to put me in a featured role, which I earned in a vocal audition.

I don't have the typical body of a musical theater performer, but directors still manage to find a place for me. I'm no longer struggling to squeeze into the typical ingénue role and have found it is much more fun playing characters with personalities. I'm a young and sexy Mrs. Claus in a Christmas show. I'm a plump and slightly neurotic Rapunzel in *Into the Woods*. I'm also spending more time teaching and directing theater and giving other fat girls like me the chance to see someone like them performing and giving them a chance to play roles other directors probably wouldn't look at them for.

It took me twenty-five years, but I'm finally realizing that I don't need my body to be validated by any person for me to be worthy of good things. I love living in my big, soft, curvy body. I love dressing it in bold colors and stretchy fabrics and fabulous shoes and big dresses. I love my breasts that bounce and my thighs that glide over each other and my booty that wiggles when I walk. I love my round belly. I love slipping my rolls into dance clothes and showing off my skills. I love what the extra weight has done for my voice, adding depth and richness that was never there before.

I never thought I would say this, but the one thing I don't miss is my 28" waist.

Elephants Never Forget

Terri Elders

My adoptive mother skittered around in high heels all day long, click-clacking around the house as she dust mopped, baked cakes, and ran the laundry through the wringer. The only times I ever saw her in flats was when she pulled weeds in the garden. Then she'd don a pair of *huaraches* and complain about how walking in them made her calves ache.

Looking back, I think Mama was self-conscious because Daddy was a six-footer and she only measured just a shade over five feet. "I'm five foot and one half inch," she frequently reminded my sister and me, emphasizing the last half of that sentence. She'd pause, and glower at us, her eyes narrowing. "And I've never weighed over a hundred pounds soaking wet."

My year-older sister, Patti, and I would exchange guilty glances. I think both of us felt sorely tempted to turn the hose on Mama, just to test the veracity of her boast. Mama must have inherited her body-build genes from her father's side of the family. Grandpa Joe, the last blacksmith in South Central Los Angeles, remained lean and wiry until he died of a heart attack in his early fifties. Her mother, my Grandma Gertie, and all three of Gertie's sisters, packed a little meat on their bones. Mama used to make fun of Aunt Cora, the biggest of the bunch, calling her Aunt Corpulent and puffing out her cheeks to mimic Aunt Cora's jowls. Even then, I wondered why it was all right to ridicule fat people.

Mama's brother had been Patti's and my birth father. While scarcely portly, he too carried around a little extra weight. And my zaftig birth mom had descended from chubbies on both sides of her family. So Patti and I had more than a little genetic predisposition toward girth.

At fourteen, I'd apparently reached my full height of 5'4", and Patti topped me by two inches. Patti probably outweighed me by twenty pounds, but I realized I no longer had the boyish figure I'd sported when I'd been an acrobatic dancer and majorette with the Carpenterettes a year or two earlier. Nonetheless, I probably weighed no more than 125 pounds, dry or wet.

Once my periods had begun, I'd noticed I was filling out a little. At first, I was pleased that I'd graduated to a larger size skirt. "I'm growing up at last," I thought, happy that I now had hips and breasts, just like the other girls in the tenth grade. Since I'd skipped third grade, I'd always lagged a little behind. Nonetheless, I'd never thought of myself as overweight, let alone fat, until one afternoon when Mama stormed into the bedroom that my sister and I shared. "What's the matter with you girls?" she demanded. "Neither of you two big elephants has offered to help dust or clean the bathroom or mop the kitchen floor. I have to do everything around here, and it's not fair. I'm barely half your size!"

Mama stabbed a finger toward the latest collection of Ray Bradbury short stories that I'd checked out from the John Muir Branch Library that morning. "Don't you have anything better to do than laze away reading all afternoon? No wonder you're getting so pudgy." She wheeled on Patti. "And you've spent the past few hours slapping on mascara. Do you think that's going to disguise how fat you're getting?"

Surprised by this sudden attack, the two of us just stared at Mama, uncertain what her point could possibly be. I always curled up with a book on weekend afternoons. And Patti always spent hours putting on makeup before going out on her Saturday night dates. Mama suddenly burst into tears. I got up off the bed and headed for the bathroom, hanging my head. I couldn't remember the last time I'd seen her cry. I think it had been when my little brother got bitten by the neighbor's spaniel.

"I'll clean the tub," I offered, fighting back tears of my own. I couldn't help it if I was taller and heavier than Mama, but it sure hurt to be called an elephant. Probably hurt just as much as a dog bite.

This incident marked a turning point in my life. Sixty years later, I still remember that at dinner that night I'd turned down seconds on mashed potatoes and I'd even skipped the cake Mama served for dessert. Obviously, I'd have to cut back on eating. Food had made me fat, and made me lazy and unlovable in my mother's eyes.

Back in 1952, nobody had ever heard of eating disorders. I'd have laughed if anybody told me they rammed their fingers down their throats to get rid of their meals. Or if anybody announced that they had to limit themselves to devouring just three stalks of celery and an apple each day. Obesity had not yet been recognized as a "disease." Even the word itself was rarely heard in those days. Nobody calculated body mass index, and cholesterol hadn't even been discovered.

Even so, I'd noticed that a few diet articles had appeared in Mama's favorite *Woman's Day* and *Family Circle* magazines, and I'd seen calorie counters for sale at Owl Drug Store. I began to check out diet books as well as short story collections on my forays to the library. Thus began my lifelong obsession with weight. I wasted decades trying one diet and then another: the Stillman diet, the every-other-day diet, the fruits and veggies with meat on Saturday diet, the avoid-anything-white diet, the AYDS appetite-suppressant candy diet. One or the other would work for a while, but when I returned to regular eating, the pounds would pile back on.

I exercised, took aerobic classes, and walked for miles at dawn, but I still remained anywhere from twenty to thirty pounds heavier than all the charts and graphs and calculators told me I should be. I was so obsessed with returning to my prepubescent weight that I even took up smoking. It's hard to realize that cigarette advertisements in those days proclaimed, "Reach for a Lucky instead of a sweet." Smoking did work somewhat in quelling my appetite, but when I quit that habit decades ago, after learning at a health fair that I'd reduced my lung capacity, I promptly packed on thirty pounds and lost a boyfriend's affection. "I'm a visual kind of guy," that man had proclaimed. "I like women slim." Of course he was an athlete, a basketball player, slim himself, descended from a mother who remained slender until she died in her mid-80s.

"Do I remind you of an elephant?" I asked him.

"Not really," he'd replied. "You don't have a trunk. And elephants are taller. And grayer."

There you have it. Even though trunkless, short, and not entirely gray, I was smart enough to figure out that this particular romance likely was doomed. I think there's more than a little truth in the adage that like attracts like.

Other than that painful exception, my excess poundage really hadn't affected my love life. I'd married early, and my first husband and I both lost and gained weight repeatedly. We divorced after twenty-five years, and then I dated a number of men of varying sizes over the next two decades. None of them ever mentioned my weight. None of them ever gagged when I took off my clothes. None of them ever kicked me out of bed.

Later, in my early sixties, I married again, a man who didn't consider body shape as the most desirable attribute in a wife. He claimed he fell in love with me the moment he read a literate email I'd sent him through an Internet dating service. "It's intelligence

I've always been interested in," he wrote. We were married for nine happy years until he died of pancreatic cancer.

Still I continued to avert my eyes from the bathroom mirror as I disrobed to hop into the shower. As I neared seventy, I found myself profoundly disappointed. I'd always believed that older women no longer fretted over what they looked like. Untrue, I learned.

"Elephant, elephant," I still heard myself repeating every time my weight edged up a pound or more. "Not good enough," I'd berate myself when I'd lose a few pounds. It was as if I still weighed my self-worth by what the scales said any given day.

Then on my seventieth birthday, I took official inventory. I toted up my life's accomplishments and then reviewed my "bucket list." What I wanted most in my remaining years was to live without feeling ashamed, guilty, and not quite up to snuff. How could I rid myself of this obsession about weight and accept my body just as it was? I wish I could say that I threw away the scales and abandoned nonfat yogurt. I didn't. I still check my weight periodically, just because I know my doctor will comment if I've gained much. But I no longer think of myself as malformed, misshapen, and all those negative images Mama and my old basketball boyfriend drove into my brain.

Despite arthritis and degenerative disc disease, at seventy-four I still do all my own housework, attend the University of Cambridge International Summer School, serve as a public member on the Washington State Medical Quality Assurance Commission, appear publicly as president of the Colville Branch American Association of University Women, and speak at writing seminars and workshops.

Recently, I conducted a session on how to write for anthologies. I read aloud from a few of the nearly sixty pieces I've published in the past five years. Nobody mentioned my weight as they applauded.

As for Mama, she had no idea how she'd undermined my self-concept. For her, a woman shaped by the values of the post-Depression era, being tiny was a virtue. Little women, after all, were easier to maintain. They didn't require so much to eat in those days when a ten-pound sack of potatoes was all my father could afford at the grocer's on payday. Mama may have initiated my obsession with my body, but I'm the one who chose to believe for most of a lifetime that I simply failed to measure up. For sixty years, I'd carted around an image of elephants that Mama had bequeathed to me. It's a relief to rid myself of resentment by choosing to absolve Mama of the legacy she left me. I doubt Mama had any idea of the harm she caused that afternoon when she first called me an elephant, as she clattered around the house in those shoes she somehow believed would add magical status to her diminutive stature.

Me, I've been a breadwinner all my life. I can afford to pay for whatever I want to eat. And it doesn't have to be low-calorie, sugarless, nonfat, synthetic food either. If I want a box of chocolates, I'll buy it.

And a rib-eye steak, too.

No Really, It Isn't Me. It's You.

Marcy Cruz

All of my life I had thought that I was the odd one because I was the fat girl in the group. Whether it was at family functions, with my group of friends, or in everyday living, I was always "that fat girl." Even when I had the moments of loathing and yo-yo dieting that most of us have experienced in our lives, I always had a strong spirit that carried me through it all and helped me to cope with feeling like the odd one out. The constant backlash and negativity from the "outside" world really just pissed me off. It made me so angry that I wore my weight as a badge of honor, my way of giving society the middle finger and telling them to kick rocks.

My anger also pushed me to celebrate my size because it made me different. I stood out and reveled in that. I never tried to hide at all. But deep down, I still wondered how it would feel to be thin. I was so envious of my thin friends because I thought that their lives were so much easier than mine. I worried about so many things: Will I fit in that chair? Does this store carry my size? Can I get on that ride at the amusement park? Will I be able to travel one day?

I never realized how much my anger hindered me in evolving

in my life. My anger made my fears multiply. Worry is an extension of fear. And I became a constant worrier, which stopped me from fully living my life. I was so blinded by anger that I could not see that other people's opinions of me didn't matter. Only my opinion of myself mattered. I spent years hearing people tell me what I couldn't do because of my size or hearing that I needed to lose weight to be beautiful. That fueled my anger even more. But instead of letting that anger push me to accomplish what people said I could never do, I let that anger build up within and create a chip on my shoulder, and it grew and grew.

Anger is like a disease that just takes over, and it is so hard to shake off once it has you in its grips. I began to isolate myself from people and drown in my anger. But the universe has a way of putting you in situations that force you to really look at yourself. I had always felt that I had a great purpose for being on this earth, but my anger was holding me back from my true potential. I needed to let go, but I didn't know how.

In 1997, at the age of twenty-seven, I started working at a corporate travel company as an executive assistant to the vice president of the company. I was terrified because it was my first full-time corporate job in Manhattan. I was fresh out of graduate school and a bit naïve in the ways of the world. I still lived at home with my parents and had just broken up with my boyfriend of eight years. He had been my first love.

One day, one of the agents came over to me and introduced himself. From then on, a friendship formed. Herman and I would go to lunch together every day. Lunch turned into our hanging out outside of work and on the weekends. Herman was my first gay friend, and I was in awe of how he made no apologies for who he was. Unbeknownst to me, his amazing outlook on life and the experiences he shared with me about how it was to grow up gay, really started to change the way I saw myself.

One day, we were discussing traveling. For as long as I could remember, I had wanted to travel and see the world. At that time, I had only been to a few places in the United States. I had only been on a plane once in my life, when I was fourteen and had visited California. So I told Herman this and he just looked at me and said, "What's holding you back? Just go." He said it so easily, like it was perfectly normal for me to go. It was in that moment that the light bulb went on. Why couldn't I see the world? Why was I worrying about traveling before even seeing if I would fit in a seat or even be let on a plane? I had been having nightmares for years about being barred from boarding a flight because of my weight. Mind you, I weighed about 295 pounds at the time and I'm 5'7". I was acting like I was so huge that I couldn't fit through the door, which was ridiculous. The anger, worry, and fear that I had built up over the years really controlled the way I viewed myself. The way I viewed myself had put all of these limitations on me.

The more I hung out with Herman and became part of his world, the more I began to slowly lose the chip on my shoulder. He took me to my first gay club where I was in total bliss around men who were so proud to be themselves with no hesitation. They accepted me with open arms. I felt like the Belle of the Ball in the gay clubs. I would be told how beautiful I was and just adored. It was truly a life-changing experience. I hadn't been genuinely happy in so long, and it felt so good to let go, be free, and just laugh. It felt good to be around people who did not judge me and my size but really saw who I was as a person. They saw my beauty even when I didn't.

Fourteen years later, Herman and I are still the best of friends. We have also traveled the world together. I have done things I thought I would never do. I still have some little traces of my worrying and fear that surface at times. But this time, I don't let that worry and fear stop me from accomplishing what I want to do. I push myself because I believe I can do anything I set my mind to. Herman and I went to Mexico City where we saw the pyramids at Teotihuacan and the Basilica of Our Lady of Guadalupe and got drunk at a tequila farm as mariachis sang to us. We went to Paris where we took a day trip to Versailles and endured rain, strikes, and my getting violently sick. We traveled to Rome where we saw the Coliseum and the Vatican and to Pompeii where we had the best pizza we had ever tasted. Then we headed to Venice where we rode through the canals and we saw artists create hand-blown glass pieces on the island of Murano.

The most profound trip for me was our trip to Hong Kong. I have an intense love for Asian culture and Buddhism. I talked Herman's ear off on the sixteen-hour flight about how I had to touch Buddha. At the Po Lin Monastery on Lantau Island, just outside of Hong Kong, sits the largest seated bronze Buddha statue in the world. However, you have to climb about twenty flights of stairs to get to the Buddha. Yes, twenty flights of stairs.

We arrived at the monastery and it was a really hot day. It was about 105 degrees, sun blazing and very humid. We stood at the foot of the stairs. I saw Herman looking up the stairs, and then he looked at me with a worried look on his face. He then said, "There is no way you're going up there. It's too much." I understood his concern. I was overweight, not in the best of shape, and it was hot as hell. I looked at the stairs and then up at Buddha. I then told Herman, "You're wrong. I'm doing it. Just make sure you're waiting for me at the top with something cold to drink."

I don't even know how long it took me to get up to the top, but I did it. People stared at me as I made my trip up because I was sweating and red-faced. But I was so determined and frankly their stares pissed me off, and that was a big motivator for me as well. Herman's telling me that I couldn't do it made me want to do it even more. I had come all this way not to touch that Buddha? No, that wasn't going to happen. That was when I knew my weight could never hold me back from doing anything I set my mind to. I was holding myself back.

Herman also inspired me to branch out and travel on my own. Once I got hit with the traveling bug, I couldn't stop. Traveling alone was a challenge because I did not have him there holding my hand or pushing me to do things outside of my comfort zone. But I felt like I had already started on this journey and I could not turn back. I did not want to turn back. I knew how it felt to live life anger-free and happy. And I did not want to lose that no matter what.

The first trip I took alone was to Club Med in Martinique. Who goes alone to Club Med? Me! I don't know how I got the courage to do it, but I did it. I was, again, the only fat girl there surrounded by thin girls in bikinis. I did not let that deter me from having fun. I signed up for a few tours and actually met some people there whom I ended up hanging out with. The trip was not perfect by any means. I have a fear of drowning but felt confident enough to try snorkeling. Unfortunately, I ended up having a panic attack and didn't do it. I was proud of myself, nonetheless, for going there by myself. It took a lot of guts to do what I did.

I went to San Francisco alone and rode the cable cars, hanging off the side of the car as it zipped up and down the hills of the city. I was determined to tackle those crazy hills on foot and walk around that beautiful town. The sight of the gorgeous Golden Gate Bridge is a memory I will always carry with me. I went to Hawaii by myself and summoned the courage to wear a bathing suit and get in the pool. I still have a fear of drowning, but I am a work in progress. I push myself a little more with each moment, and I am not giving up on the dream that one day I will swim in the ocean fearlessly.

I went to London, Paris, and Amsterdam alone and spent two weeks there. I met up with a friend in Paris, who went to Amsterdam with me. But most of the trip, I was on my own. I remember being so stressed out in Paris because I did not know the language. This was my second time there, but I was without Herman this time. I actually got off the metro midway into the city, sat on the platform, and had a moment. In Paris, I was stared at a lot, and it was hard to deal with because, for a while, I had forgotten how it felt to be scrutinized like that. So I had my moment and just pushed forward. I got to see the "Mona Lisa" and have my *Da Vinci*

Code experience, go to the top of the Arc de Triomphe and see a marvelous view of the city, and navigate the metro on my own. I felt pretty fierce.

I realize now that during all those times that I felt like the odd one out, I was probably the most normal person there because of my acceptance for who I was. It makes others uncomfortable to see me comfortable in my own skin. Once I accepted that it wasn't me who was the problem but other people, my view of the world changed instantly. I always think of that Buddha moment when I encounter something that pushes my limits. We will always have those twenty-flights-of-stairs moments in our lives. But it is how we decide to tackle them that counts.

So when I look at the picture taken of me on the Sky Walk at the Grand Canyon, I wonder why it took so long for that happy fat chick to come out. I had no idea what I was missing in this world, and now the sky's the limit. And I didn't have to lose weight to get to this place of fabulousness. Who would've thought that could happen? So thank you, Herman, and thank you, World, for bringing out this amazing, kick-ass chick that was always there but was just waiting for her moment to shine.

PART 2

LOVE

Love is resilient and strong. It can withstand mistakes and errors of judgment. It can handle that time you only ate carrots and low-fat Pop-Tarts for a week, and it was still there after that time you stood in front of the mirror—lipstick smeared, spit bubbling, wailing loudly—promising yourself that you'd never, ever go on a date again. You can come to know love, grow love, and recommit to and relearn love whenever you are ready. There's no such thing as the perfect way to love. We come to love and experience love in ways that work for us; there is no such thing as nice and tidy. We are born with the capacity to love, but make no mistake: Love is a skill. It is something we learn to do every day.

Sometimes it's the kind of thing that's messy and makes your mascara run. Sometimes it makes you feel calm and secure. A lot

of the time, it feels elusive, frustrating, impossible. In this section, you will read about all kinds of love: the love between a mother and a daughter; the love of the self; and the deeply visceral, moan-inducing, dirty kind of love. And a note on the "visceral, moan-inducing, dirty kind of love": Love and sex aren't separate beings, arch enemies, estranged neighbors! Sex (with yourself or with a few people) can inspire wonderful feelings of self-love, even if it's the slightly-awkward-yet-hot kind you have with boys from the bar. Love lives in sweet words and knowing glances, orgasms and kisses, fights, fear, and forgiveness. It lives in the mistakes, the drama, suspended in the "space between." Love is never as far as you think, and it is scary and big, weird and wonderful.

The Fat Queen of Speed Dating

Golda Poretsky

Back on that muggy April evening in 2006, I wasn't the fierce fatty that I am now. This was the "Before Time," before my fat era, before I knew that calling myself fat could be a great thing, before I heard of Kate Harding or Paul Campos, before I devoted my life to being a Health at Every Size counselor. I was just a plus-size late-twenties lawyer who was looking for a few good men to date. And so I found myself at a nondescript Soho bar at a Speed Dating for Young Professionals event.

I got there just as the event was about to start and took a quick scan of the room. There were the usual speed-dating suspects—men in suits looking bored, women with impossibly flat-ironed hair wearing the latest Banana Republic offerings. No one other than me was wearing the latest Lane Bryant dress, and I had a feeling that most of these women wouldn't know what Lane Bryant was if you asked. I caught a glimpse of a tall, broad-shouldered guy in a really well-made suit, who my brain registered as "hot," but I soon shifted my attention to the event organizer, a compact, blond young man with thespian mannerisms who was motioning to me to get signed in and take a seat.

The first round of speed dating went by in a blur. Apparently, the event was overbooked, so we only had three minutes to talk with each guy before he was off to the next table. Three minutes is absolutely no time to get to know anyone, but it's also the perfect amount of time to get to know someone when you realize that you instantly dislike him. Most of the guys were friendly but sort of nondescript. I was supposed to be taking notes on each of them so I would know which ones to check off at the end of the night, but I started losing track after Dude #4.

The weird thing was I actually *liked* speed dating. Just a few months before, I had come to the conclusion that I had to start changing the way I thought about myself and my life. Until then, I had held every negative, horrible belief about being fat and dating that one could possibly believe. I believed that for someone to date me, they would have to get past my fat. They would have to love me in spite of my fat. The idea that someone could be attracted to all of me was something I couldn't even consider. Every time I went on a jdate or an okcupid date or a match.com date, I went in with the expectation that the dude would be disappointed.

Then something started to shift for me. I still hadn't heard of fat acceptance or body acceptance, so, instead of starting to accept my body for its own sake, I made a different sort of crazy decision (or what seemed crazy to me at the time). I decided that I was going to focus on having fun. I was going to seek out fun in every aspect of my life. I was going to seek out the fun in different experiences. I felt that if I could focus on fun, I would attract more fun and I'd be happier.

The amazing thing is that it actually worked. I started to have more fun dating (and trying on clothes and looking at myself in the mirror). When I went on a date with someone new, I decided to have fun with that person. If they wanted to have fun with me, the date went well. If the dude wasn't feeling it, that was his problem. It was an incredibly healing thing to come home from a date that didn't go so well and not feel like your prodigious belly was the cause.

So, as a result, I was actually enjoying speed dating, and the first round flew by. After I'd met ten guys in about thirty minutes, the organizer called time and told us we'd have a ten-minute break. Knowing that there would be a rush on the ladies' room, I said a quick good-bye to my last date and made a run for it.

I didn't really need to use the bathroom, but I like going to the bathroom to get away from it all. I like the privacy, the moment alone to think my own thoughts. I often let my mind wander and forget that I'm actually supposed to be somewhere. So I was sitting in the stall, pondering away, when a group of women walked in.

"Did you meet that guy, Bill, yet?" the woman in the red heels said.

"Which one is he?" the woman in the black heels said.

"The big one in the suit. The cute one. He works in television," Red Heels said, as if she learned it from pillow talk.

"Oh, yeah! He was hot!" Black Heels agreed.

"I hope he checks me off," Peep Toes chimed in.

"I hope he does more than that!" Black Heels whispered.

I felt like a fly on the wall in that ladies' room (even though there were actual flies who might have disagreed with that assessment). It seemed that Bill was the guy they were all after. Bill was the guy that everyone wanted to be checked off by. Bill was the tallest monkey, and we were all hungry for impossible-to-reach bananas.

When round two started, Bill was the first one to sit down at my table. He smiled and I smiled back. You could tell he was tall and big—he seemed almost unwieldy behind that tiny little bar table. He was wearing a really nice suit, and his dark blond hair was straight and cut pretty short. His shoulders were hunched in a little, in a shy, almost protective way.

He seemed like a man of few words, so I started the conversation with the only thing I could think of to say. "I was in the ladies' room earlier, and everyone was talking about how they want you to pick them," I said, instantly regretting it. I get three minutes with a guy, and I'm going to talk about the bathroom?

"Oh, really?" he said, leaning back a bit. "I'm probably not going to pick any of them."

I was kind of surprised. A lot of the women in the first round seemed like the kind of women *every* straight guy seemed to like. And if online personal ads were to be believed, didn't every straight guy want a petite, athletic woman with straight hair who is as comfortable wearing jeans to a Yankee game as she is wearing a ball gown? I could imagine Black Heels, Red Heels, and Peep Toes meeting these important criteria. "Why not?"

"They're not really my type," he said, with a smile.

I nodded slowly and knowingly, but not really knowing what he meant. Then the bell rang, and it was time for Bill to move on. I assumed that I had totally blown it with him and decided to focus my attention on Dude #12.

After all of the women had met all of the men, the event organizers handed us a list and asked us to check off which people we wanted to go out with. If you checked off someone who checked you off, you would get an email with their contact information. I looked at the long list of guys and felt less than hopeful. I met about twenty guys that night, but the only one I really wanted to go on a date with was Bill. I checked off one or two guys who were fun to talk to, but Bill was kind of it. I only wanted to go out with the guy that everyone else wanted to go out with. I was a cliché. I was picking the big, tall guy because he could reach the highest bananas.

After the official speed dating ended, a number of the participants had moved over to the bar to have another drink and talk and insist that "this is my first time speed dating!" even though it's probably statistically impossible that everyone at every speed-dating event has never speed dated before. I was grabbing my jacket and bag slowly, not sure if I was going to stay for a drink and talk about speed dating or go home and blog about speed dating, when I heard someone yell in a deep baritone, "Golda, come 'ere!"

I wheeled around and saw Bill surrounded by five women (only two with identifiable footwear) as he leaned casually against the bar. I felt like everyone's eyes were on me as I walked from the back of the bar to the front. The women who had encircled Bill begrudgingly made room for me. I felt incredibly awkward, like I wanted to take each one of these women aside and say, "Seriously, I'm not in competition with you. Let's all be friends." Bill started asking basic things about me, where I lived, what I liked to do for fun. It was clear that he wasn't interested in the other women.

It turned out that we lived not too far from each other, so he asked if I wanted to share a cab. I agreed at once. He took my hand and said, "Let's get out of here." And we did. The fattest woman in the room had just left the bar with the guy that all of the other women wanted.

Things fizzled out with Bill after a few dates, but it didn't matter. (I had started dating two other guys at the same time, but that's another story. . . .) That speed-dating experience allowed me to see that I couldn't (and shouldn't) assume that being fatter than other women was an impediment to my dating life. It allowed me to realize that attraction is rarely as cookie-cutter as we're led to believe. I finally realized that I could be totally hot and attractive because of the way I looked, not in spite of it.

BBW Party

Tigress Osborn

The first time I heard the term *BBW* (Big Beautiful Woman), I was a chunky high school girl. I was the only Black girl in the honors program at my school. I lived in the ghetto away from my suburban classmates. I wore a size 16 when everyone else seemed to be a size 6, and I just felt different all the time. I know most of us felt different all the time, but at sixteen, everyone else seemed to fit in when I stood out. I wanted to shine, to be me, to be unique. (Think Denise Huxtable with better grades.) But I also wanted to be part of something. So I was attracted to things that included me in a group. I read every novel in my public library that was written by a Black woman. I discovered a magazine for mixed race people at a bookstore in a nearby town. And I read *BBW* magazine because I was a Big Beautiful Woman-to-be.

I liked the term *big, beautiful woman*, and I was attracted to friendships with other big girls because they understood the woes of my fatness, and they also liked to shop with me in plus-size stores. In college, a couple of my best friends were plus-size sistas, and after a high-school life of being one of the biggest girls (or at least I thought I was) and one of the only brown girls, it was nice to have big, brown friends. Together, we began to discover a sense of identity around our size in the same way we were growing as women and as Black women. At our school's diversity day, we met a woman from NAAFA (National Association for the Advancement of Fat Acceptance) who introduced us to the idea that there were people who were just fine with being fat, thank you very much. I had only seen such things articulated on *Donahue*.

I came from a family of big, beautiful women, and some of them were sexy and sassy and full of bravado, but even the most confident of them were always talking about dieting, and the rest expressed nothing but embarrassment and hatred about their bodies or pretended their bodies didn't exist. My friend and I decided we wouldn't try to lose weight; we'd try to accept ourselves. That "commitment" eventually deteriorated into stopping the insanity with Susan Powter and doing aerobics with a Jody Whatley workout tape in the basement of the cultural center. I never lost a pound until starvation came as a side effect of my early-twenties depression, but I never quite gave up the idea that I should be losing weight at all times. I swung back and forth between being a proud young BBW and wishing to shop at 5-7-9.

Growing into adulthood, I moved to California to be with my first love and discovered myself in a place where diversity meant people of all skin tones and sizes and lifestyles and politics. My grandfather had once said California was the land of fruits and nuts, and I found that I liked these fruity, nutty folks and their not-Arizona ways. But I still felt too big. I had learned to accept my size—in theory. I should be able to be whatever size I want because that's not what matters most about me. In reality, I could look at other fat women and see beauty, but I thought I needed to get a little smaller to be more attractive myself. Not skinny-skinny, just without this belly.

The partner I loved through my twenties got bigger every year and so did I. We were homebodies, hitting the movies every weekend and going to a comedy show or concert once in a while. I liked clothes, but really didn't have anywhere to wear them but work. My social life consisted of going to IHOP with my best friend from college. I thought I was kind of cute, but didn't really think it mattered much. I would always be in the shadow of women like my gorgeous Coke-bottle-shaped coworker when it came to beauty and attraction, so I better focus on being fierce in other ways. Said ferocity caught fire when another colleague forwarded me and about fifty other people a "joke" that involved several Photoshopped horrors of what celebrities would look like if they gained a couple hundred pounds. I fired back an email to everyone on the list saying I identified with those women and didn't think my body was a punch line. No one responded, but I didn't care. My coworker never told a fat joke in front of me again, and I started a website called Big Girl Pride that was part blog and part resource list for fat girls.

Meanwhile, my partner dieted and exercised, lost and gained. He was a big guy, but I was a fat lady, and in addition to the weight I carried, I carried a lot of guilt for not having a body that he was more attracted to. My fat girl self-acceptance was stumbling along, but I was doing a lot better at accepting other people's bodies than my own. I was working on being a proud public BBW, but privately, I lived with a man who wouldn't touch me anymore because of my rolls. I once teased him that I would do an erotic dance on our solid pine coffee table for him. He said I might break it. Today, I would take the chance and tell him he better enjoy it for as long as the table could stand it. Back then, I swallowed that comment, ate some more ice cream, and internalized my anger for another year or so.

When one of my oldest and dearest friends found a lump in her breast, I swallowed that news, too. I was afraid that talking about my fears would give them more energy, make them more likely to actualize. So I didn't tell anyone but my partner. Every morning when I got undressed for my shower, I found myself looking at myself in the mirror. Even as I struggled to accept big me, I still thought of my breasts as just another big part that made me look fatter. I wore a lot of v-necks, but that was as much because I didn't like cloth on my throat as it was to accentuate my figure. I wore minimizer bras because taking inches off any part of me was still on my agenda. But Susan's news turned out to be the worst, and all of a sudden I had a new perspective. I had a healthy and beautiful body that was going to waste because I loved someone who didn't love it. Someone I loved was losing her breasts. I had to learn to love mine, dammit.

My body had been on hiatus sexually (well, at least on hiatus from sex with another person. I am still a Scorpio, after all, so some things just had to be taken into my own hands). But at the same time, I was learning to love my body in a whole new way. I signed up for a sixty-mile breast cancer awareness walk, and the required training taught me to think of myself as an athlete for the first time since my adolescent track-and-field experiences. I walked miles every day, got stronger legs and tougher feet, and shifted some fat around but didn't really lose weight. I met one of the greatest friends of my life in response to online whining on a local listserv by other walkers who'd received extra-large shirts when they needed small ("And why would they even have all these extra-large shirts? This is an athletic event!").

My self-made family was growing. I felt good in other parts of my life and proud of my physical accomplishments. I loved what my body was doing, but I hated what it wasn't doing. I grew restless. That restlessness led to the decision that I'd rather be single with the hope of someone loving me, fat and all, than be ensconced in a lifelong relationship where I didn't have to be alone but I had to be celibate. I left my partner after almost a decade of loving him. I felt terrified, but free.

Single-girl world was where the term *BBW* began to have great meaning in my life again. I had no idea how to date, so I did what we do these days and turned to the Internet. Craigslist was free and fun to peruse. In my new little apartment by the lake, I sat alone with my new laptop, instant messaging my college BFF and searching for ads from people looking for fat chicks. I had not yet discovered the existence of men who like all kinds of women, and I naïvely believed there were two kinds of guys in the world—regular guys who, of course, liked thin women and the (I thought then) much, much smaller number of men who actually liked fat women best. Stepping into the dating world, I began to see that there were men who had very strong preferences for one size or another, but there were also men who could see beauty all over the spectrum of size. I quickly learned that *BBW* was the online dating world's best search term if I wanted to find men who would like my body . . . or if I wanted to identify men who wouldn't touch me with a 10-foot pole. Online, fat girls are both reviled and revered. Searching *BBW* often led to ads clearly stating that smaller was better, ranging from "no disrespect but it's just not my choice" to straight up "no fat chicks" sentiments. I later discovered the exact same thing was true (at least on Craigslist) if I wanted to date women.

I also discovered the existence of a whole social world for people of size. I was starting to explore nightlife, and my experiences with being a big girl in mainstream nightclubs were bittersweet. I discovered that I liked being out on the town, getting dressed up for cocktails and dancing, sitting somewhere pretty with my girls and cool drinks in martini glasses. I was still learning to believe I was attractive including my body, not in spite of it, so I was surprised to get looks and smiles and winks. But when traveling in a fat girl pack, there were whispers and giggles, too.

I had vague memories of hearing about BBW dances, and I had a colleague who'd told me about a BBW party back when I was common-law married and staying home most weekends. Now that I was out in the world, I decided to start checking these things out. I met an awesome group of girls through a house party advertised on a BBW social group, and some of them turned out to be regulars at a local BBW club I'd been very curious about.

Soon after I began attending that event, another opened nearby. I continued attending mainstream parties. I observed the pros and cons of both environments and wished for the ambiance of San Francisco's hot spots but the warm welcome and wide seats of the fat girl parties I was attending with my new friends. I must've talked about this even more than I realized, because I came home after a particularly frustrating experience out on the town and my roommate listened to me complain for a while until he finally said, "Why don't you just start your own party like you keep saying?" I didn't even remember having said that, but his words burrowed in. I kept going back to the absolutely ridiculous idea that I—a late-blooming me who never even went out until my thirties—could become a nightclub promoter.

The more I went back to it, the less ridiculous it seemed. I'd planned all kinds of events in my career. How different could a party be? One of my best friends was working for a small record company at the time, and I sought his advice on the behind-the-scenes questions of DJs and venues and getting the word out. Within two months, I'd made informational interview dates with the folks who ran the existing BBW parties I'd been attending, and I sat down with them to talk about community, mutually beneficial and friendly competition, and supporting each other if I decided to launch another party. Both teams gave advice and good wishes. Two more months later, with the help of some friends, a MySpace page, and a logo that probably looked like the Photoshop experiment it was, Full Figure Entertainment debuted. I didn't always know what I was doing, but I had a vision of fashion and fun and glamour and good feelings.

By day, I'm a diversity educator and because I don't know how to turn that off, my vision also included empowerment, inclusion, and celebration of all the ways the Oakland/San Francisco Bay Area is diverse. Three and a half years later, Full Figure Friday is a bimonthly hip-hop party that attracts all races, various sexual orientations, and bodies from stick-thin to tree-trunk-thick to proud f-a-t. Our website and social networking sites get thousands of hits each month from across the United States and from many other countries, and our party has been featured in local media and on French television and the BBC.

So here I am at thirty-seven, over twenty years after sticking my toe in the pool of size acceptance by flipping through a magazine called *BBW*, now running a BBW party. I had no idea how much Full Figure Entertainment would come to mean to me or how much it would change my life. I especially didn't know how much it would come to mean to other women, not just as a party, but as a community. It is absolutely surreal to have gone from being a fledgling fierce fatty struggling to accept myself to being a role model for women all over the Internet and all over the world. Once, another BBW party promoter told me that BBW parties were just that—parties, not movements. I think about that all the time. Like it or not, creating a space for people who are often marginalized means that people who needed that space will look at you with gratitude and for leadership. Knowing that what I feel about my own body is now relevant to people outside of my skin is both scary and inspirational. From long-lost high school friends found on Facebook to total strangers whom I'll probably never meet in person, I get asked questions from where to buy a good bra (my minimizer days are dead and buried) to how to deal with a spouse's fatphobia. I answer from the heart, admit when I don't know the answers, and share my own stories. I remind people that we are all in it together and that, yes, I still struggle with my body sometimes, too, even if I am on a nightclub flyer in stilettos with a pack of gorgeous plus-size models.

But I struggle a lot less often than I used to. Being around so many other women who consider themselves BBWs and wear that identity with confidence helps regenerate my own confidence when I'm feeling doubt or frustration or fatigue from battling fat girl stereotypes and big girl barriers. *BBW* was once just a euphemism for "fat chick" to me, but now, because it is the term that so many women identify with and find pride in, it has come to represent community for me in a way I never expected it would. I like to use the word *fat* because it's unapologetic and political. But I like *BBW* because it's the term that first introduced me to the idea that fat women could consider themselves beautiful and say so with pride. I have learned, after all these years, to include myself in that vision of big beauty instead of seeing it as something other women could be but that I never would be. Now, I count myself among the beautiful, too, and I surround myself with BBWs who embrace that title. Full Figure Entertainment is a party and a movement, and I'm proud to be the conductor of that train. Maybe I inspire the BBWs who come along for the ride; certainly, they inspire me.

And if that's not a reason to party, I don't know what is.

2Fat2Fuck

Rachel Kacenjar

When I was fourteen, I decided I wanted to have sex. I didn't really realize what sex entailed or what I was getting into, I just knew I wanted to have it. I was tired of just thinking about it all the time—obsessing over every little detail. How would I feel during? Would it hurt? What would I be like afterward? What if I got pregnant? Would I instantly be in love with whomever I had it with? If I just did it, this Dear-God-It's-Me-Margaret neurosis would stop, wouldn't it?

Because the Internet was really new at the time, my answer to everything was "library!" The library was where I had learned about things like Satan and the effects of marijuana. Though I locked myself in the children's reading room and sat in a pile of guides to women's anatomy and Kama Sutra books one afternoon, I still didn't find the information I was looking for. Sure, these were drawings of my coochie and drawings of people in positions, but how did they even get to that point? I stole a *Playboy* from my father and tried to self-teach. To my dismay, I opened it up only to find models in provocative settings and poses, but no actual sex. I hadn't realized until then that *Playboy* was about pretend sex and pretend women. I thought to myself, "Who are these women?" They didn't look like any women I knew. And as much as I found them shiny and fascinating, this just wasn't the how-to I had been seeking. This learning experience had proven to be a total fail.

I tried to think of anyone I possibly could that I could talk to about having sex. I grew up hanging out with an older girl that my mother had called *promiscuous*, but at the time I didn't know what it meant, and we had stopped hanging out because she got pregnant. It'd probably be weird to call her after three years of noncommunication, right? "Hi Alice! How's your toddler? Did you ever finish high school? What's a rim job?"

All of my other friends were virgins, but I was willing to be a pioneer. My brother was a huge dork, and definitely knew more about computers than vaginas, but he was a senior and had a long-time girlfriend. So I figured he'd done the deed at least once after a school dance or something. It took me days and days to work up the courage to pose my burning question to him. We sat stoic and noncommunicative in our divorced parents' 1970s basement— orange-and-green shag rug, wood panel walls, red velvet wet bar, stone fireplace and all.

After school one day during the last commercial break of a *Seinfeld* episode, I turned to him and asked, "How do you know if it's the right time to have sex?"

"Why do you want to know?" he snarked.

I looked down at my Sketchers, scared, awkward, seeking compassion.

"Don't worry about it now, Rachel," he said.

I looked at him, seeking.

"You're too fat to fuck anyway."

While many young girls would find this phrase traumatizing, I simply let my eyes glaze and watched the end of the episode. I had been told I was fat and/or ugly nearly every day of my life for at least the seven years or so preceding that moment, so it sounded boilerplate to me. And let's face it, my brother was probably right. TV and movies never had fat sexy women in them. In fact, I couldn't think of one fat and sexy woman I knew. Were most fat women not getting laid? That didn't seem fair or true! And though his brush-off of my question annoyed me, I can't say my brother's words hurt me; in fact, they inspired me. I had come head to head with adversity before, and I was the type of righteous babe who liked to prove folks wrong. I would indeed prove that I was *not* too fat to fuck. In fact, I was quite fucking fuckable. I just needed a little work.

To proceed with this mission, I would take a few actions (imagine a montage sequence, like when Rocky beats up the hanging meat and jogs in the arctic preparing for battle).

Action Number 1: I would hang photos of fuckable women on my refrigerator to remind me not to eat and procure some humiliating exercise habits. I had seen this keen trick proven effective on *Melrose Place*. I couldn't commit to a healthy diet if I wanted results, so I'd stick to liters upon liters of Diet Dr. Pepper and one half of a fat-free Pop-Tart twice a day regimen. I had learned tricks such as these from a group my mother signed me up for when I was twelve years old. It was a community group for obese teens, and although I was not a teen (and probably just overweight and not obese), my mother made sure they'd make a special exception for me. God forbid I be a twelve-year-old that was complacent about her chubby, growing body! There had to be an intervention! Twelve years old, 5'4", and 150 pounds? Unacceptable! The group was made up of eight other young women who all outweighed me by 100 or 200 pounds. Though not quite reliable, I thought they were all pretty cool chicks, but any kind of meeting that weighs you upon entering would never be my type of meeting. To get out of the whole thing, I began to starve myself and go for hour-long jogs every day before school in the eighth grade. It made Mom happy; it seemed like my "diagnosis: death" of obese had shifted to just slightly overweight. Mom could sleep easier at night, but more importantly I could avoid her nagging, guilt-laden bullshit.

While I took easily to jogging in the morning (it wasn't too hot, it was dark, and I could secretly smoke cigarettes behind the condo development when I was done), it was boring, and the results came slow to my body. Extreme measures had to be taken! My BFF had a trampoline, which seemed like an obvious solution, right? We'd get high with the gay kid on the bus after school, put garbage bags over our bodies, go outside in the nearly 90-degree heat, and jump up and down until our brains died. This same BFF showed me how to slam your stomach at just the right angle into the kitchen sink to coax recently swallowed food out of your belly.

Action Number 2: Dress sluttier. While I had been tall for my age for a while, all the other girls had finally caught up and surpassed me. I thought to myself, "What areas can I enhance to surpass their royal giraffe status?" My face was okay—nothing truly stellar, though I often heard "You'd just be so pretty if you lost weight!" Maybe some red lipstick? Who doesn't like makeup? That was doable. Hmm, what else? I certainly didn't have a nice ass. In fact, I didn't understand the appeal of an ass. Wasn't it just the meeting point of two legs put together? We pooped and farted out of our butts; I couldn't imagine sex with a hole dedicated to feces. Wait, I knew the answer. Duh! Boobs were definitely the key. While mine weren't of any real stature, one could acquire miracle contraptions to turn any type of titty into an eye-googling jug. I would return the virtual cornucopia of sickly fruit-scented Victoria's Secret lotions that I had received for my birthday back to the store and purchase a "Miracle Bra" with my profits. Cleavage got you to second base, I'd thought, but miracle boobs would probably at least solicit a finger-fuck.

Action Number 3: Actually socialize with boys. I already had a kind-of boyfriend. He was so dreamy, long black hair like Dave Navarro, nice body, nervous laugh. He wore heavy metal T-shirts and played both guitar *and* drums. I felt so lucky to have such an awesome guy. We would hang out on the weekends at his absent father's house and dry hump for hours. We didn't talk much at school though. He usually seemed really busy with his friends. If I really wanted to prove my level of fuckability, I would have to not only get him to fuck me, but also fuck some of his friends, and maybe even some older guys to inherit the technique I desired. I was always a quick study and an honor student. So it wouldn't be that hard for me to learn how to really please a man. If you're going to do something, do it well, right?

It didn't take long for my three-prong fucking plan to take effect. In fact, the Tuesday after I had spent the weekend coordinating new slutty outfits out of clothes that I borrowed from my thinner BFF to wear with my Miracle Bra and blood red Wet 'n' Wild lipstick, I had already had two guys in school slip me sexually obligatory notes. One of them was my kind-of boyfriend, in which he blathered on for lines and lines about a new song he was working on that was about me and ended this missive by asking, "ARE YOU READY YET?!" He meant ready to fuck, and my honest answer was "yes." He was quite pleased to hear the news.

That whole week I thought about what might happen. Would he wear a condom? Should I buy them? Did I have to go to the gynecologist now that I'd be a "woman"? What if my pussy smelled weird? Was it supposed to smell fishy, or was that bad? What if he saw me naked and thought I was gross? What about the stretch marks on my tits? What if I jiggled when we fucked? What about my gut? What about my thunder thighs, or worse yet—between them—my pubes? I was supposed to shave them off, right? I'd have to shave my legs and paint my toenails! What if I suffocated him when I mounted him? Did I have to find something sexy to wear to distract him from my fat rolls? Were you supposed to wear lingerie under your clothes or change into it? What if he wanted to do it in a weird position? I didn't know the names of all of them. What if he proposed a position and I didn't know what he was talking about?! Maybe I should have kept that Kama Sutra book from the library.

Maybe I should try to watch some porn. Maybe this whole fucking thing was a lot bigger and scarier than I had thought. These possibilities and ideas overwhelmed me, and the constant questions annoyed me. So much so that when I tried to masturbate and think about it, I'd get so anxious that I'd never get off. I'd get so frustrated, humping the pole of my canopy bed over and over, trying to get excited, but really, I just wanted to get this whole de-virginizing ordeal over with.

Before I knew it, it was the end of the school day on Friday. I had never felt more nervous in my entire life, and ninth period, Sociology, had never dragged on so long. I was on the brink of becoming a woman, for chrissakes! I mean, I had my period already, but once you didn't have a hymen anymore you were really a lady. I went home and prepared with a night of shaving, waxing, painting, starving, and sit-ups. I practiced things I'd say by watching pornos and repeating: "I love your big, juicy cock!" (I'd have to pretend it was a chili-dog or something to say that with a straight face.) "Let me rub those sexy balls!" (Did women really think balls were sexy? I didn't see the appeal.) I picked out the most user-friendly dress and a front-closure bra. I stole two condoms out of my brother's drawer just in case. I was ready.

The next night, stud muffin and I had just finished up with about two hours of clumsy, over-the-shirt making out when I couldn't wait anymore. "Are we ever going to fuck?" I asked, somewhat annoyed, but mostly anxious. He smiled, taking off his stonewashed jeans. "Hell yeah," he laughed. He struggled with his jeans, as he hadn't taken his Air Jordans off yet. I watched him, feeling sorry for him, as I *knew* this was the first and last time we'd have sex. My brother was right. I was too fat to fuck. Once he saw my body, got one look at my puffy, chubby vuh-jay-jay, it'd be over.

He started to unbutton my shirt. As soon as he unbuttoned enough to expose my teenage breasts, he stopped. I prayed to God, whom I didn't even believe in, that he wouldn't unbutton any further than that. If he could just focus on my miracle boobs, maybe he wouldn't notice the extra thirty pounds I had brought into bed with me. He was hard, grinding his tight-whitey–clad pelvis into my jean skirt. He thrust his hands under my skirt, and for the first time ever someone else's hand touched my vagina. I gasped, excited at the new sensation. I felt his other hand slide up my shirt, caressing my belly fat. I began to giggle, nervous and scared.

"I'm so ticklish," I laughed, lying through my teeth, wishing with all my fucking might he'd take his hands off my fat. "You're so hot," he said. With disbelief, I put my hand into his underwear. His penis was a lot smaller than I had expected it to be. It somehow felt bigger through his pants. He got on top of me, and I was grateful. I didn't want him looking up at me half-naked; the lighting was too bright, and I'd be in danger of an explosion of exposed flaws.

"Is this okay?" he said as he grabbed a condom from his nightstand drawer.

"Yep," I agreed. I looked up at the ceiling and stared at the texture. Popcorn ceilings were so popular in our town of 1970s houses. I'd come to stare at nearly twenty more of those ceilings during the pre-coitus time delays spent in my youth.

I was rudely awakened from my calming ceiling-staring by a jab somewhere near my butthole. "Ahhh!" I reacted. I used my hand to forgivingly guide him inside me. I looked at his contorted face. It seemed like he was possessed. I felt his naked stomach slap against mine, create suction, and make a fart noise. I immediately felt humiliated, but he didn't seem to notice. Before I could re-affix my eyes to the popcorn ceiling, I felt him enter me. It didn't hurt like everyone said it would. I mostly just felt relief. Was he doing it wrong? Before I could ask, it was over, as he oooh'd and aaaah'd like he just saw the Virgin Mary herself, wearing gold lamé, singing show tunes on top of a piano.

That was it? I spent weeks and weeks of my life preparing for less than a minute of nothing?

I smiled as he climbed off of me, as I realized something then that changed me forever. You could never be too fat to fuck.

Guys were so caught up in their boners and their own ejaculation-oriented world when they fucked you, they wouldn't even notice if you transformed into a sheep dog when you were fucking, so they certainly weren't going to notice my flaws. This attitude set the precedent for the next several rounds of fucking. This time, I'd go for sophomore guys, or even older guys who could fuck longer. I'd learn to advocate for myself and teach guys where to touch me. I stopped wearing the Miracle Bra—it was uncomfortable. I started eating again, and getting up early to jog was out of the question if I was up late fucking. Guys didn't care about my flab or my jiggle; they just wanted pussy. Why did women try so hard? Men are so eager and easy. If their dick was inside of you, you were gorgeous to them. It was a given.

At least twenty-five fucks later, I was sixteen. I loved sex, and somehow food tasted better than ever, too. I was fatter than ever, and I fucked more than ever. With my hot, older, submissive, steady boyfriend, with other guys, with girls even. I fucked without shame as I ate without shame. Fast-food restaurants and teenage boys catered to my secret alike. The Arby's by Dave's house didn't know I had just gone to the McDonald's by John's apartment, and McDonald's wouldn't know if I went to Burger King ten minutes later, just as John wouldn't know if I went to Jake's. I could eat whatever I wanted, alone in my car, my battering ram that plowed down my shame and replaced it with trans fats while ushering me to my next sex appointment. I could fuck in there, too! And just like the boys I fucked—the boys that would never have the balls (for the record, I never did find out what the appeal of balls was) to tell their friends (the same friends who were also fucking me) that they were getting pussy from a fattie—my secrets were safe and mine, all mine.

Consumption of all things fueled my pig + pussy tour of my small town. Eating and fucking, fucking and eating. These were things I could control. These were things that fulfilled me. These were actions I was supposed to be ashamed of, but I wasn't. I felt revolutionary. I felt like I had a secret that other girls couldn't have. I felt invigorated by the glory of my body and its power. Maybe I'd been fucking around for the wrong reasons, or shit, maybe they were the right ones. All I know is that I learned to love my body by letting other people love my body. Even if it was selfish, or just to get off. Even if they just loved me with their dick or their mouth, or their fingers and not their hearts, they still accepted me—somehow, some way. They always seemed to have an easier time accepting me than I did. I look at pictures of myself now from back then, and I wasn't even fat. I was fleshy, glowing, young and gorgeous.

And I certainly wasn't—nor will I ever be—too fat to fuck.

Dear Sweet Body

Alysia Angel

Dear Sweet Body,
    You are a temple. You are pillars of past, walls of art, high-arching doorways of history. You are a place of worship for some and a place to rest weary heads of others. You are for everyone who comes by you honestly and with intention and love. You are racing lines of stretch marks and roundness for grabbing. You are tense wires of electricity spanning across continents of admirers. You are small and compact and yet expansive and wanting. You ache to be touched how you like it and send out warnings to those who might not. You are witch spells in the mouth of caves.

    You are the ocean, your great waves undulating seductively around massive wooden ships. You woo sailors with glints of shiny trick lighting and the sound of sirens in your shallows. You are massive and deep and salty at all of the right times. Your tide pools tremble with tiny discovery. You are the moon as it fattens, stretching out and wrapping itself in mist for seduction purposes. You are the moon that calls to the sun, waxing and waning just to show off. You are the salty-lipped beach trip, red bathing suit and round thighs soaking in admiration and sunshine.

You are a journey. You are smooth brow and heaving heart. You are saddle ass and sweaty thighs and hard memories wrapped in the finest swatches of silk under heaving breasts. You demand that cartographers with years of experience simply find the terrible softness in your hips, your lips, and your collarbone. You are unraveling miles of surprising shyness, teeth biting into pillows of lips. You are unending. Would-be suitors shade their eyes on horizons of your equator. Knights send messengers ahead to beat out the others.

You are a wild horse. You buck easily. You tame rarely. You run until you are a sheen of sweat and lust. You toss your head at danger and leap over obstacles. You are youthful and old and always free. You belong to no one. You like being asked, and you love giving it away to the worthy few. You are orgasmic, plentiful, more than enough, and ready. You are feral when cornered, and you know you can be used as a weapon in moments of danger. You are surprisingly fast when you need to be and viscous like honey when the moment begs for it.

Sweet body, you are a carriage, a mystery, a puzzle, a long road ahead of me. You support me and rarely protest when I make you do things you would rather not. You house all of my soul's history sweetly. You make tears for when the pain is too much or the happiness spills out. You are healthy and whole, rarely sick or out of order, but instead always open for business, poppies out on the sidewalk to prove it. You are cavity-free in the teeth, with no bone ever broken and phantom bruises that sometimes tingle and then are placated by new stories and new layers.

You are still glimmering after four wars. You are the dazed smile on my lover's face when asked to disrobe. You are the sun singing against you in your racy red bathing suit. You are the truth of standing up straight like your Papaw always told you to. You are steel beams covered by marzipan, coated in maple syrup.

You belong to no one, and yet your arms open to many. Your fist remembers revolution. Your hips undulate to faraway beats. Your thighs part to receive. Your mouth pants. Your heart swells and aches for everything.

Sweet body.

You are a beauty.

Love,
Alysia

Voluptuous Life

April Flores

I entered this industry very gradually, at my own pace, by participating in several projects over several years. I started off doing erotic modeling for Carlos Batts (who is now my husband) in the year 2000. We met at a gallery opening where he approached me and asked if I would be interested in modeling for him. I had always loved to be in front of the camera, and I was really attracted to him, so I said yes. He was working on his first book *Wild Skin*, and I eventually had the honor of being on the cover of it. Looking back now, it is really funny because I had only been the subject in photographs for a few friends. When I told my mom that I was going to be taking pictures with a stranger I had just met she warned: "Be careful! He is going to put pictures of you on the Internet." I would have never imagined that my relationship with Carlos, and my being a subject and performer, would grow as far as they have.

When we first met to discuss the shoot, Carlos told me that he wanted to shoot me in a bikini. At the time, I was not completely comfortable with the idea of being photographed in a bikini because

I had never done anything like that. However, I didn't want to let my inexperience get in the way of trying something new. I was also flattered and excited that an artist drew inspiration from me. During our first meeting, he said that he wanted to change the world with me, and we have been working toward that since then.

Carlos and I had a wonderful creative chemistry, and I became his muse. We shot constantly, while always trying to push new artistic boundaries. The one constant element in our relationship was the camera, and eventually Carlos started shooting me with a video camera. Slowly we started to shift the focus onto the moving image as opposed to the still image. He started filming more than shooting stills and began to write our first film, *Alter Ego*.

During that time, Carlos shot Belladonna for a Japanese magazine called *Warp*. He suggested that she and I take pictures together for our ongoing book project. She said she liked my look, and we set up a meeting. During the meeting, I was instantly drawn to her genuine, sweet demeanor. She asked if I would be interested in shooting a sex scene for one of her movies. I had never even thought of ever performing in an adult film, but once again I was up for a new experience and said yes. I honestly thought it was going to be a one-time thing, and I was only motivated by wanting to experience something new and exciting. That, and I thought she was really sexy! We shot and our scene was in her movie *Evil Pink 2*.

Most of our friends are artists, photographers, and performers, and about eight months after my first shoot, a friend who was directing her own film invited me to perform in it as well. The shoots after that came more frequently, and before I knew it, I was shooting about once every other month, which is more than I had ever set out to do. I have been really lucky because most of the time I have been able to work with friends and people I respect and admire. I have tried to create work that I can be proud of and that represents women, specifically plus-size women, in a positive way. Unfortunately, some of the footage I shot ended up in films that have degrading titles, but that is the reality of what can happen when you sign a release. The producers can use the footage in whatever film they want, and once I have signed, it is out of my control. When determining whether or not to participate in a project, I take into consideration who is directing, what company it will be for, how I will be portrayed as a woman, and if it will challenge me to grow as a performer.

Maintaining a catalog of mostly sex-positive projects is so important to me because my main goal with my work is to show people that size should not dictate happiness or limit you from expressing and enjoying your sexuality. I am trying to challenge the norm of what is thought of as beautiful and sexy. I want other women to see what I am doing and be inspired to explore and express their own sexuality regardless of their weight or size. I also want people to challenge their own ideas of beauty. I am very blessed because I think my body of work has had a good influence on women, couples, and even men. Getting feedback or reading emails from people who have been positively affected by seeing my work or reading an interview I have done is the best feeling ever!

The industry was very welcoming and accepting of me. Because there are so many niches in adult film, there is a more open mind for people of all sizes performing and participating in adult films. Within the adult industry, I think I am seen as a performer who maintains a certain work ethic and who has tried to create a voice and a more positive image for big girls. I myself have seen many changes. When I first started out in 2005, the BBW sites I saw mostly showcased a very specific type of person. The models were all exactly the same in body size and ethnicity. There wasn't a significant range or variety of body sizes represented that we as plus-size women inhabit. Over time, I have seen a greater range of body sizes and more women of color being featured in adult sites and films. To me, it is clear that more women are feeling empowered by expressing themselves in a sexual and exhibitionistic way. I really hope that my work has had something to do with this change I have seen.

In 2008, I was contacted by Topco Sales about the possibility of creating a sex toy. It was very exciting for me because this became the first sex toy ever molded from a plus-size woman's body. The molding process was very interesting. It was cast directly from my body at the Topco offices. They have a whole process they have perfected. First, they prepped my skin with a Vaseline-type cream. They then added a blue creamy substance over the desired area to be molded. This substance was really warm and felt great. Once this concoction hardened, they carefully removed the mold revealing my body's negative. At that time, they also molded my face which slightly freaked me out. I was doing great at first, but it became unbearable once everything was applied and started to harden. Feeling the weight of the materials on my face, not being able to move, and having only two small holes to breathe from was a little too much for me. My body got really hot, and I kept repeating *immortalized* in my head. It was all over after five minutes or so. The whole day was completely surreal and an amazing experience.

Some people see the toy as the ultimate form of objectification, but I don't see it that way at all. I am proud that I provided the "parts" for this and see it as groundbreaking. I am proud because the toy was created out of a need and a void that existed in an industry that has usually focused on sex toys based on thin bodies. I think the creation and success of the toy showed not only fans, but also corporations that there are people who desire plus-size women and that there is a real audience for products that represent a broader spectrum of body types. The toy has sold really well, and my second toy which is a "stroker pussy" was released in 2012.

Another great thing that came from the toy was "The April Flores Toy Show," which was an art show that my husband thought of and curated. Carlos and I always try to mix art with sex, and this was a great way to demonstrate how art and sex come together and enhance each other. It was also a unique way of using sex toys in a nontraditional manner to provoke thought and conversation. In this exhibit, the toy cast provided the blank canvas on which each artist expressed a vision. The cool thing about the show was that it was an unusual format in which to explore issues such as beauty, sexuality, pleasure toys, and art. The show exhibited in Los Angeles twice, San Francisco, New York, and Philadelphia. Artists from each city the show visited were used, which caused the show to evolve and incorporate elements of each of these cities as well. The artists put a lot of thought into their pieces, and each made a unique statement. I was excited by their participation and willingness to use a nontraditional medium as a canvas.

My work in porn has given me the opportunity to grow as a performer and as a woman. Because of my work in this industry I've also had the privilege of meeting and becoming friends with some of the most genuinely wonderful people. I like that porn has allowed me to explore my sexuality in ways that I never dreamed would be possible. I have enjoyed pushing my sexual boundaries; being able to do that while indulging my exhibitionist tendencies has made me pretty happy. I hope my work is perceived with respect and an open mind, and I hope that my work continues to challenge people's preconceived notions about what it is to be a plus-size woman.

Women with Big Bellies

Ashley Young

Hen House

As a child, I already knew what shape my body would take. There are generations of us: women with heavy breasts, oval-shaped bellies, and wide, firm thighs. I called our home "The Hen House"—a three-bedroom apartment where my mother, my grandmother, and I lived throughout the duration of my childhood. Our home was a place where men were seldom seen. So our bodies were never objectified or shamefully covered but quietly celebrated. And their nakedness was the shape of my future.

My mother had the habit of walking around the house naked. She'd undress in stages: her shoes and jacket at the door, her suit coat and skirt in the living room, and her underwear and bra in her bedroom. Between my grandmother's room and the bathroom, she bore only her birthday suit, a caramel-colored configuration of circles that composed her 5'0" frame.

My grandmother took her baths with the door open. The day she called me in to wash her back, I had never seen a body sag with age like hers. Her breasts were deflated, and her left nipple scarred from her long bout with cancer. They sat atop her shrinking belly and rested on her thinning thighs. Her back was smooth to the touch, as smooth as her 72-year-old barely wrinkled face.

In between their nakedness, they shared one set of clothing primarily composed of my grandmother's purchases. My mother would stand in front of Grandma's closet trying on suit after suit before work each morning. She'd parade around our apartment like she was in a fashion show with my grandmother's outfit commentary accompanying the sounds of her heels clicking on our hardwood floors. They'd always complained about how ugly big women's clothing was, so much so that my mother joked that the Women's World plus-size section at the mall ought to be called "Women as big and equally as ugly as the World." She thought the clothes looked old and frumpy, but my grandmother was always dressed in the best church clothing and my mother was learning to follow her style. I always thought they both looked beautiful when they left the house in their patterned dresses and matching jewelry sets, but it was clear they felt most comfortable at home and naked.

At five, my tummy poked out a little but when I lay down it went flat. My only fancy outfit was my kindergarten uniform. Grandmother wouldn't let me run around the house naked, in fear I'd catch a cold, but I figured when I grew up, I'd walk around naked like them. They looked proud with their bellies out, and I only hoped I could be so bold when I grew up. I knew I'd form their same round tummies when I hit puberty, so fat was inevitable, and coming from the Hen House, I was sure I'd be prepared.

Fat Jeans

Puberty came much earlier than expected. I was in fifth grade, and it was only a few weeks into the school year when I got my period. In what seemed like overnight, I had C-cup breasts and a two-week heavy flow. And I was fat—too fat to fit into clothes in the girl junior's section at the mall. Between my thighs, my hips, and my tits, I was officially a plus-size girl.

My grandmother's famous macaroni and cheese didn't help. I loved her home-cooked meals, and since the start of my period, I had been craving chocolates and candy like crazy. My grandmother was happy to let me eat dessert after dinner. All the women around me were celebrating my new monthly visitor while I was still trying to adjust to pads, bras, and cramps. I quickly outgrew all my clothes from the beginning of the school year. I mourned for a while when I discovered I could no longer fit into my favorite pair of Paris jeans and was forced to face the fact that I would be shopping in The Limited plus-size line for teens.

The big-girl teen section at Macy's didn't have as many choices. Even though I could fit all the clothes, the pants were always too long or too stretchy and the shirts were sometimes too loose. My mother would often hem my jeans too high and turn my pants into high waters. If I wanted to show off my new cleavage, I had to wear a shirt a size too small and sacrifice having to suck in when I noticed my stomach was sticking out.

It was the 1990s and bell bottoms were back in style. Most of the girls in my class were skinny and wearing light-washed jeans with flared bottoms below tight-fitting pink and blue baby T-shirts. We were all preparing for middle school next year and assumed we should get a head start on showing off our budding bodies. But my body was getting in the way of joining my classmates. My stomach was too big to show off, and they didn't have bell bottoms in the plus-size section.

I suddenly had the body of a fourteen-year-old, and I was starting to learn that precocious puberty was a bit of a gift and a curse. With little effort on my part, my body automatically made me both visible and different. I was slowly becoming one of the fattest girls in my class, and though all the girls wanted breasts, they certainly didn't want a stomach. My clothes fit awkwardly on me as my body continued to change, and I never felt like I could fit in with the new fashion trend. I was starting to get attention from boys, but the ones my age would just look at my breasts dumbfounded, too nervous to work up the nerve to actually talk to me. The older guys who gawked were just plain creepy.

I was learning that as a fat girl I had to make compromises. I had to try to fit in with a very different body and begin to find some solace in my fast-track puberty, as I knew it was only the beginning. I had to figure out what clothes I felt comfortable in, and I knew I had to develop some self-confidence if I was destined to a life as a plus-size chick.

Desperate to fall in line with the rest of my peers, I searched every square foot of the mall with my mother, hoping to find a pair of bell bottoms that fit me. I settled on a pair of brown stretch pants with flared bottoms that deceivingly posed as jeans. I wore them with a pair of platform Sketchers sneakers and rolled up my baggy shirts to show off my thighs. I was excited to finally be falling into fashion, but bell bottoms quickly wore out their hype, and I went back to my outlandish plus-size dresses.

The week I began my first sex-ed class, I discovered I wasn't the only girl in my class with her period. Kari was a thick girl like me, with a fat face and large dimples that pinched each cheek when she smiled. I considered her one of the cool girls who wore baggy shirts and jeans. All her clothes were high-prized brand names like FUBU and Sean John. I was never really into brands, but she always looked like a comfortable, cool, tough girl in all of her outfits.

One day when I asked our teacher if I could go to the bathroom, Kari noticed me shoving a pad in my pocket. I hadn't told anyone about my period—at this point, the cause of my body mutation was my best-kept secret. When Kari caught me in the hallway alone, she pulled me aside.

"Are you on your period?"

I could barely say anything, shocked she'd noticed the pad.

"I saw you slip the pad out of your desk. It's okay," she said in a whisper. "I just started my period, too."

We both smiled at each other a little, and in the empty hallway, we talked about how we hated having to sneak around the classroom for our feminine products. I whined about my cramps, and Kari groaned about how fast her body was changing.

"How big are your breasts?" I asked her, excited to be able to talk to a girl my size.

"38Cs," she said, in an even quieter voice.

"No way! I'm a 40C," I said. "Man, doesn't it suck so much to buy clothes?"

"Yeah it does, but I shop with my older cousins 'cause they're all fatties and know where to go to get their gear," she said, her dimples forming in her cheeks when she smiled. "It kinda sucks to be a big girl, but you'll get used to it."

She gave me a little shove, and I smiled back at her.

We agreed to keep each other's secret, and Kari invited me to her house to try on her clothes. We never got really close, but after our fat girl gab session, I felt like I had joined some secret club for big girls. I decided my body fat wasn't so bad after all.

Naked Girl Time

The first woman I fell in love with was plus-size.

We met in college at a student audition for *Hair: The Musical*. What first attracted me to Jordan were her curves. She had wide thighs that were accented by her dark, painted-on jeans. Underneath her gold-and-black disco-ball shirt was a thick, flat tummy and strong, broad shoulders pushed out from underneath her sleeves. She reminded me of my middle-school image of a cool girl, with her clean black-and-white Adidas and trendy sports bag. I loved the way she stood solid in her body and her round face bore the whitest, most enthusiastic smile.

Having only recently embraced my attraction to women, I was eager to fall in love with Jordan. Before we knew it, we were a couple—blasting the radio on rides through our college town, staying up until sunrise talking about our futures, and learning to love each other's bodies. We were both big women, and as I grew to love Jordan's body, I started to love my own.

I learned her body's geography quickly. Even in the dark, I could map out the curve of her back and memorize the folds of her hips and thighs. Soon we stopped making love in the dark, and when we were too tired for sex, we'd lie in the light and look at each other. There was so much of her body to explore and so many experiences our big bodies shared. Jordan regaled me with stories of Fat Camp and years of learning to accept her body. We giggled about our speedy descents into puberty and tried on each other's clothes. We talked about the body parts we loved and the ones we didn't.

"I'm not a huge fan of this upper butt fat," Jordan said as she guided her hand from her lower back to the top of her backside, "I mean can't the fat just shift itself so I can have one of those bouncing Black-girl booties?"

"Oh, whatever, I love that part of you. It holds up your jeans," I said with a giggle. "I think my tummy is getting way too big."

I pinched some belly fat and made a pouty face. Jordan moved my hand to steal a firm embrace.

"I love your belly," she said, and started kissing the stretch marks on the surface of my stomach.

We started calling those body sessions "Naked Girl Time"— unclothed moments where we could vent, bitch, and remind each other that our bodies are beautiful. Naked Girl Time has spilled over to our everyday home life. Four years later, we are still barely covered, talking for hours like giggly school girls.

During these times, I remember my fat-girl origins. I am just as round and brown as my mother and grandmother, undressing all over the house: bottomless the minute I walk in the door and topless as the home hours wear on. I am reminded that I come from women who taught me that being in a full-size body is an amazing space to define my womanhood.

And that nakedness is the best place to grow.

Journeying into a Fat, Fleshy Vulva

Shawna Peters

When I think back to when my fat positivity started, I seem bombarded by memories. But these memories are filled not only with pride but also with sorrow. And like all memories, they are mediated by what I want to remember and what I want to forget. As a fat woman, I want to suggest that this process of remembering may never feel solely like an engagement with fat positivity, as my experience of pleasure as a fat girl is both reparative and painful. Without remembering and acknowledging the anxiety and self-hatred that I had toward my own body as a fat girl, the reparative feelings that I have now for my own fat flesh would never have felt so clear. So let us not dwell on either/or binaries but instead recognize the vastness of fat girls' experiences with sex, masturbation, and pleasure; these memories are not only spaces of celebration but also spaces of trauma and healing. This is my attempt to remember how my fat shaped my own understanding of my sexual embodiment. I am sharing this in the hopes that some fat women may find some solace in reflecting back on their girlhoods and that in the future, fat girls will no longer feel that they have to hide their sexual selves or their bodies but rather embrace them with confidence.

I was in the closet, but not about my gender identity or about my sexuality. I was in the closet about my non-normative body size, and more specifically about my vulva. Just as Eve Sedgwick and Michael Moon have asked "What kind of secret can the body of a fat woman keep?"*, as a fat girl, the secret I was keeping was not about my self-confidence or that I was fat affirmative, but that not only were my chin, my arms, my belly, and my thighs fat, but my vulva was fat, too. Even though we assume that fat is hyper visible on the body, my vulva was something I could conceal. Most of the time I felt that I could even give the illusion that my vulva looked like thin women's and thin girls' vulvas. When my friends would make jokes about fat women's camel toes or fat women's paunches, I would suck in my fatness for as long as I could and then I would proceed to hide the fatness of my belly and my vulva under tights, long shirts, or long dresses. I hoped that in hiding parts of my fat body, my vulva could pass as normative and, therefore, desirable to myself and to the world.

Then after finishing high school, I joined the V-Day campaign at my university, a feminist antiviolence campaign, or as it is more popularly known, the organization that fund-raises through the production of Eve Ensler's *The Vagina Monologues*. I recall during my second year as a volunteer and actress that some young women in the campaign would tell personal stories about their vulvas or even at times show each other their vulvas in a backstage bathroom or in a backstage hallway. This was not necessarily a sexual act, per se, although it may have been, but I seemed to envision this exchange as an act of mutuality, curiosity, and awe. I remember feeling extremely vulnerable in these exchanges because I had no desire to show my vulva to anyone but myself and even then that

---

* Eve Kosofsky Sedgwick, The Epistemology of the Closet (Berkeley: University of California Press, 2008), 218.

was seldom. Surrounded by what seemed like happy confident vulvas, I was hiding my fat vulva as a stand-in for my internalized fat phobia. At the time, there was no room for me to reclaim my vulva because it seemed that for me to do so I would have to reclaim my fat. I continued to keep my vulva contained and invisible so that no one would notice that down there I looked different. I felt like a hypocrite for being able to speak politically about violence against women and the violence that becomes institutionalized when we silence women's experiences about their vulvas and shame women about their sexuality. However, despite my participation in deconstructing silence and shame, I was still sitting in silence and disavowing my fat in shame.

Then one evening, there began a shift in my consciousness. I only hope that all fat girls should be so lucky. Thanks to the V-Day organizers, I signed up for The Myth of the Vaginal Orgasm workshop that they organized at a local women's sex store and emporium. The woman giving the workshop was loud, charismatic, and quite blunt. She was not quite thin but not fat either. As twenty of us sat around in a circle, she offered us chocolate-dipped strawberries and began educating young folks about female pleasure organs.

At one point, a timid young woman put up her hand and asked if, more or less, all vulvas looked the same. At first, the woman spoke with authority by saying yes. Then she changed her answer and said well, no. She started describing vulvas by stating some folks have bigger and smaller labia and different-size clitorises and how some vulvas may not look like vulvas at all. Then she stated, "fat women's vulvas have more cushion here and may face slightly down" as she demonstrated by putting her hand on her flesh, below her belly button onto her lower abdomen. At first, I felt sick to my stomach as this woman had just revealed what I had been hiding: my puffy, fat vulva. And then, I felt acknowledged. This woman said these words without contempt or disgust. She simply stated that fat women have different-looking vulvas and that was that.

Even if it was momentary and insignificant to most of the people at the workshop, I felt that my body had been recognized.

In that moment, I stopped sucking in my belly and exhaled for what felt like the first time. This was a momentary glimpse at what fat positivity felt like and I wanted to be immersed within its grasp. During the rest of the workshop, I nibbled on a chocolate-dipped strawberry and I savored with excitement what I had just heard. After the workshop, I timidly bought my first vibrator. It was red, like the strawberries, and after the transaction went through I thanked the woman for everything and quickly walked home. I went immediately back to my apartment, snuggled into bed and opened up my legs.

I started slow. Reaching down with my fingers across my soft round belly, through my fine curly hair down to my cushion. I placed my hand on my fat and started curling my pubic hair around with my finger, and for a moment, I forgot every fat insult and fat-phobic joke that had hailed me into place that week. I moved my finger down through my soft silky flesh and moved through my layers upon layers of labia, spreading apart my lips to a kind of fleshy utopia. I had traveled here before but had never felt so much clarity, so much recognition, and so much happiness from feeling my fat. It was like I was lost in my body for a moment, and it was here that I could begin to resignify my own vulva as something genuine and something intimate. As my fingers moved beyond my outer labia and into my inner labia, my fatty tissue was warming up to my touch. I reached further down into my fat and graced my clitoris's presence and moved my fingers down to my wide open vagina. I entered myself, and my cum was like a cup of lemon gelato that had been sitting in the sun all day. I moved my fingers clockwise and counterclockwise, and I moved my left index finger back up through my folds and onto my clitoris. I rolled my fingers around in a slow circular motion as if my clitoris was an unknown planet and I was orbiting around it without a care in the world. As I caressed around harder and harder, I began to sweat and take pleasure in my sweating and in this exercising. If only my fat-phobic gym teacher could see me now. I was sweating and sweating and panting and panting and taking such delight in finally being good at a sport. I sweated through my full-bottom underwear, through the straps of my bra, and through my shirt onto the sheets. The revolutions became faster and faster until the bulges of my thighs were quaking, and then I stopped.

I reached for my new sexy purchase, turned it on, and put the rounded crimson bullet between my legs starting at the base of my vagina. As I pushed the vibrator further and further inside, the vibrator was soaked in my sweetness and my cum flooded out onto my sheets and down my vagina to my anus. I moved the vibrator up toward my clitoral hood and pulsed on my clitoris moving my bottom down toward the ground and then up toward the ceiling. As the pulsing pushed up against my soft fatty flesh, my thighs started trembling and my toes started curling. My breathing became louder and louder and breathier and breathier, and like a wave from the Mediterranean, I clenched my round belly and my fat rumbled and shook and twitched until I came. As I turned my vibrator off, I entered a kind of sweaty peaceful slumber. My fat fleshy vulva oozed with delight at the evening I had had. In that moment, I was not disavowing my fat flesh or hiding it in shame. I was a sexy, cumming fat body, a body that took pleasure in orgasms, in sweating, and in loving fat flesh. This memory allows me to recall what it feels like to appreciate fat flesh and how pleasurable fat flesh can be. I have learned to appreciate fat, no matter where it is on the body or how much fat we have. For me, my fat folds have become complex and messy and beautiful.

This memory, in particular, sustains me whenever I am feeling alone or I am feeling that my own internalization of fat phobia is overpowering my feelings of fat pride. I am able to escape to this memory when I want to feel acknowledged and sexy and loved, and for that, I will always be grateful for that woman's words at the workshop. My journeying within fat positivity has not been an easy one, not that I would assume anyone's ever is. It has taken me years of surrounding myself with a loving feminist and queer community to realize what it means to reclaim your body, your orgasms, and your world. And even now, fat positivity as a part of practicing self-love and self-care is not without its ambiguity. I am daily faced with feeling like my belly, my chin, my arms, and my thighs are too fat for this thin-privileging world. But my orgasms are still mine. My orgasms are full of fat pride as they are like little moments where my fat layers can open up and find solace in every fold. Every time my fat vulva orgasms, I feel like I am challenging the fat-phobic ideologies that teach us that fat women are asexual, unattractive, and undesirable. Every time I orgasm, I know I must unlearn these dominant discourses and think about fat differently. My orgasms have become my own fat feminist utopia, where my world momentarily transforms, and this utopia is not fat phobic and not plagued with a moral panic around body size. This is when my fat can become the source of my pleasure instead of the source of my pain, and I feel at ease in the world.

For the fat girl who has yet to avow her fat vulva, let her be so lucky as to find fat-affirmative folks in her life who allow her to see that fat girls have a sexuality and that she can own that sexuality as hers and hers alone. May fat women teach fat girls that the road to self-hatred is not an easy one to be on and, rather, fat positivity may offer glimpses toward an alternative route to bodily being in this world. Fat positivity may allow fat women and fat girls to redefine their fat folds as sexy, desirable, and joyful parts of our embodiment. We must learn to live in them and love them and have alternative places where we can travel to to revel in their glory. Wherever your fat-positive place may be, in your orgasms, your community, your guitar, your paint brush, or your family, keep this community close so that the folds in your body know that you are loved and that you are truly flabulous.

Fat on the Beach: A Mother's Battle Cry

Christa Trueman

One of my earliest memories is of being at the beach with my mother and some of her friends. This was in Ontario in the late 1970s or early '80s, and going to the beach was a big event that happened only once or twice a year. Lake Ontario was not considered swimable; it was Lake Huron that got all our summer business. So there'd typically be an hour or more drive involved, with a car crammed full of coolers and inflatables and blankets and excited young adults.

On this particular day, I remember lying on my towel in the hot sunlight, beads of water evaporating off my skin, my hair lank and damp around my face and ears. I was sneaking glances at my mom, who was lying, dry and fair, on her towel next to me. She was on her back in a bikini, her long blond hair shining, the cooler full of beer and sandwiches positioned so as not to block any of the light from kissing her skin. She would jokingly complain she never could get a tan, just lots and lots of connected freckles. My mom had me when she was seventeen, and she was a beautiful young woman— a single mother who entertained a number of unsuitable suitors through my childhood. This day at the beach was an anomaly not only because it was such an event to get to the beach in the first place, but also because, as a single mother with an active dating life, it was very rare for her to have the time for us to engage in one-on-one interactions.

I was a fish at that age, and while the lure of the large lake waves was nearly overwhelming, the desire to be near my mom was greater. I don't think I was more than four years old. I was certainly not in school yet because I recall most of my days were spent with sitters who planted me in front of their rabbit-eared television sets with a ketchup sandwich (my favorite) for lunch time with *Sesame Street*. We had brought some sort of game with us to the beach . . . or maybe a book to read? And I remember asking my mom if she would play the game or read the book to me. And something about this activity was going to require that she turn on her towel, so that she was lying on her side (maybe so she could shuffle the cards? or show me the pictures?). And I was completely baffled when she said, "No, we can't do that right now, honey," because she wasn't busy doing anything else—just lying there. There was no man around to capture her attention. All the guys that had come along were tossing flying discs or footballs yards away in the sand. It was her day off from work. We were finally alone, just her and me—the perfect chance for us to have fun together.

"But why?" I asked, not hurt or petulant, just curious.

She didn't even look at me through her sunglasses, just stayed motionless on her towel as she said, "I can't roll on my side right now. I'm in a bikini and if I go on my side, all my belly fat rolls will show."

I remember looking down at my own body—pudgy with natural protective layers of baby fat tightly encased in a one-piece swimsuit. I was lying on my side and Mom was right . . . my belly *was* pooching out a little onto my damp towel. If I had other questions about this turn of events, I can't remember; I don't think I did though. I think I just accepted her words at face value. Lying on your side on a towel at the beach was risky or even wrong. It's a small thing, really, when I look back over my childhood, teen years, and young adulthood and all the messages I got over the years about fat, weight, and body shape and size. Certainly one could argue that the restricted-calorie diets I was put on in my 'tween years had more of an effect on my developing disordered eating patterns than this one small incident where my very young, very vulnerable, very beautiful mother expressed concern about her own body and its fat rolls to me. Certainly one could argue being told by endless adult males in my life that I was "too big," "shaped wrong," "looked like a quarterback for the Dallas Cowboys," had "huge tits for a twelve-year-old," "could be as pretty as my cousin if I'd just stop eating chips like it was a race," and on and on had more to do with my cultivating a self-loathing so deep and burning that I tried to destroy myself, directly and indirectly, over and over again before the age of twenty. Certainly being shamed by doctors, school nurses, and gym teachers about my lack of physical fitness (which in retrospect was ridiculous; I loved running, biking, gymnastics, roller skating, climbing, and all those outdoor games neighborhood kids would play together) had more to do with my learning to hide myself away, not make myself a spectacle in the gymnasium or at the track than my mother making some offhanded comment about her dissatisfaction with her body.

My mother wasn't abusive about my body size either. Oh, I'm sure she worried about me as I hit puberty and started to get fat, as any parent worries that their child will suffer from teasing or bullying or shunning for being different. And I know that the low-cal diets and entreaties to get me exerting myself physically (once I figured out you could beg your way out of gym class with a well-timed "I have cramps"—coupled with a forearm across your abdomen—I basically stopped participating in PE at all) were coming from that place of concern and love. But that one incident, the one where my lovely, slightly curvy but never even really pudgy and certainly not fat mother said she couldn't play a game or read a book to me at the beach because turning on her side would show the world her belly fat rolls, has stuck with me my entire life.

It used to be what my mind would turn over and over and over when I'd go to the beach as a teenager. First of all, I wouldn't have been caught dead in a bikini. Secondly, I knew from this early lesson that my job at the beach was to lay out my towel as quickly and as flat as possible, then lie down on that towel as quickly and as flat as possible. If I had to move for any reason—to sit up to get a drink, to stand up to go to the public washrooms—it was of vital importance that I first pull a T-shirt on over my swimsuit. Any bending of the torso in any way, shape, or form at the beach or swimming pool was sure to expose my secret, my shame, my belly fat rolls. No one must ever know about those.

This went on for years, despite the fact that I have always loved the water, the beach, a lake, and the ocean, and despite the fact that exerting myself in the glaring summer sun and then rewarding my hot flesh with the icy splash of a natural body of water is one of the most exquisite, greatest joys I can think of in this life. I spent the better part of the first half of my life feeling unable to enjoy these simple pleasures because so much of my thought processes and energy were spent trying to keep people from figuring out I was fat.

We can excuse my mother, for she was only reflecting what her culture had put on her from the moment she realized there could be a wrong way to have a body. And we can also excuse her because she was barely more than a kid when she had me, and who reading this can say that they, at age twenty or twenty-one, had enough understanding of feminism and body politics and self-esteem to really not care if some people at the beach see their belly fat rolls? Hell, who can say that at age thirty? Forty-five? Eighty? Not many of us, I'd wager.

But here's the rub. Yes, hearing about how I must hide my belly fat rolls at the tender age of four or five obviously deeply affected me and contributed to a long couple of decades where I fought so hard against loving my body. But as I slowly became more radicalized in the fat-acceptance movement in my twenties, this memory became less of a reminder to hide, and be ashamed, and more of a reminder of why we must fight, fight, fight against the shame and resist the urge to hide.

At the age of twenty-seven, I gave birth to my daughter. I'd already had a son, four years earlier, and so it wasn't the act of becoming a mother that completed this transformation for me; it was the fact that I was suddenly aware of the immense responsibility I now faced in the raising of this new human girl child. I knew that while my son would face his own issues with fitting in, sexism, and body type, the pressures my daughter was about to fall under—starting very young, very, very young, from the moment someone first decides she needs a frilly pink dress and a ribbon in her hair—could make or break her.

And I thought back to that day at the beach with my mother. I thought back to my cute little poochy four-year-old tummy going from just something that was a part of me—with no subtext whatsoever—to something that I needed to hide. I looked at my own infant daughter, who was only a few years away from her very first message that there was a wrong way to have a body in this society, and I decided right then and there that this message was not going to come from me.

I can't say for sure what my daughter's earliest memories of being at the beach with me are going to be like. I am certainly much fatter than my own mother was and have been my daughter's entire life. I stopped making myself lie flat on my towel in the sunshine for hours at a time, unless I feel like taking a hot sunny nap. I do often cover up at the beach but only because skin cancer killed my grandfather and I find sunburns unpleasant, not because I am trying to trick anyone into thinking I'm not as fat as I am.

I love the beach now. I love running into the water, my entire body jiggling, all that fat showing, no way to hide it. I love shrieking and laughing and having splash fights and lifting and tossing my girl into the waves as she shrieks and laughs right back at me. I love sitting up on my towel, my hair dripping, my belly resting on my lap, as we share our picnic basket and futilely try to wipe sand off our potato chips. I love that my daughter sees me this way: fat and happy, fat and swimming, fat and lying on my side on my towel next to her, reading her a passage out of my book or flipping over a card in a game of Crazy Eights. I can't guarantee that she is going to get through her teen years unscathed by our body-shaming society, but I can guarantee that she's going to have me in her life as the counterpoint to all of that. And any time I get those twinges of shame—because they do linger, and they do still inhibit me—I recount that day on the beach as a small girl with my own mother. Only now it's not a reminder of how my belly fat rolls are not okay.

It is a reminder that my belly fat rolls are a battle cry.

Fat Sex Works!

Kitty Stryker

I am a fat girl.

I'm also a hot girl, a clever girl, a sweet girl, an evil girl, and many other things.

But none of those other words seems to make people writhe uncomfortably in their seats as the word *fat*. Fat is an insult in the United States, where I grew up, often used alongside insults to intelligence and hygiene. When I started calling myself fat as a way of combating my own prejudices about the term, I was (and am) constantly told how I'm a Big Beautiful Woman, that I'm just curvy, that I'm pretty, not fat—like you can't be both.

But I actually *like* the word *fat*.

Fat implies fruitfulness and richness. It's succinct. It allows me to take up space, and I feel less and less like apologizing for it—not to my family, not to my friends, and certainly not to my clients.

You see, I'm a sex worker. I make my living with my body, knowing how to use it best to tease and please myself and the people I work with. I take glamorous photographs, wear fancy clothes, and generally partake in the highest of high femme. It's not something

I could have imagined feeling comfortable with ten years ago. I was anxious enough taking my clothes off in front of lovers, never mind expecting someone to pay me for it.

I used to be a really skinny kid—tall, lean, tomboyish. I took karate, ballet, and swimming lessons regularly. I wasn't comfortable in my body then either. I was kind of awkward and gangly, with crooked teeth and no idea how to do my hair. Then I hit puberty, got braces, and exploded out all over the place like a sponge dinosaur.

With the breasts came hips and thighs. And then I was on medication that added water weight and more hips and more breasts—which, of course, being a socialized female, made me into a bulimic. Not that bulimia helped with anything, ultimately, except for making me feel like I had some weird control over my body. Instead, I gained a fair bit of weight, leading me to generally hate my body, which, sadly, is par for the course when you're a woman, especially in the United States. I felt pretty terrible about how I looked, wanting to hide under baggy clothes and slumped shoulders.

Don't get me wrong: I dated and I had lovers here and there, but I remember feeling nervous about my ability to keep them, feeling like they settled for me 'til they got someone better. I didn't believe I could be sexy. I had a couple of partners who told me that I was a BBW, that I should feel comfortable and sensual in my body. Slowly, I began to trust and believe them. I started to wear lingerie and make an effort with makeup and doing my hair. As I got more comfortable with my body and moved to San Francisco, I played around with the idea of becoming a sex worker to help me get through school. Juggling two jobs and classes was overwhelming, and I enjoyed sexuality in all forms. So why not give it a go, I figured.

In spite of my highly sexual energy, becoming a sex worker came gradually, first as a professional domme, then as an erotic masseuse, and finally as a prostitute. I started with the area of sex work I believed would judge me the least for my size, as I saw professional dommes of various body types, ages, and personalities. For some kinky people, I could be the ideal mistress, with my ability to push them around, smother them with my luscious thighs, my hips and breasts exploding out of a corset.

Getting clients was a struggle because I was a fat girl. I learned pretty quickly that I would have to put up with a lot of bullshit on a daily basis. A woman I worked under wouldn't tell clients about me because "who'd want to see you?" When I went independent, there were phone calls from wannabe clients I had spoken to on the phone, felt uneasy about, and had refused to see. One man told me I was a fat cow and that he didn't want me. Another stalked me online and via text for six months, saying things like, "Isn't it interesting how many hookers are found dead each year?" He tried to friend me on Facebook. That sort of harassment was just part of the job, I figured. I wondered whether it would be this abusive if I continued to do sex work.

The first break I got was when I started using the term *BBW* on my ads and site. Before then, I used *curvy* or some other euphemistic term. When I used *Big Beautiful Woman* instead, I got more questions, more interest, more . . . letching. But the difference was that these men tended to be more interested in—how did one term it?—my fleshy ass and plump pussy lips than in me as a person, which is when I realized that *BBW* wasn't just a description; it was an invitation to see my body as a fetish object itself. And I wasn't—and am still not—sure how I feel about it. I guess it's like anything: a boy who talks to my face *as well as* my tits and ass makes me feel adored. A boy who *only* talks to my body makes me feel like a breathing sex doll. That's not size related. But it's this weird, cold detachment they project onto me that makes me feel detached, like this body isn't mine. It's uncomfortable and strange.

It's not just in my type of sex work; I think that fetishization applies to the visualization of fat female sexuality generally. For example, as much as I like that there's mainstream fat porn on the

Web, it's usually offensive and humiliates the subject. And there's still the attitude behind the scenes (and sometimes in front of the camera) that fat girls are worth less than other models. One of my favorite kink websites unfortunately never hires women bigger than a size 12—as far as I can tell—despite the kink scene being more welcoming to fat than many other sexual spheres. When I went to a women's event that was being filmed, the camera barely looked at me, despite the fact that my partner is a model who has worked with them before. And BBW is listed as a fetish on sites like FetLife (http://www.FetLife.com, a social networking site for people interested in kinky sex, dating, and friendships). I'm trying to work out if declaring oneself as a BBW is actually a thing of pride or just seen as an invitation for people to perv out over my thighs.

It's frustrating beyond belief to not only have the normal bits men get obnoxious about, but also extra fat for them to ladle their commentary onto. You can always wear a T-shirt and jeans to hide other bits, but you can't do that with your size. And this objectification isn't just sexual—oh no, I can't count the number of women who have asked about my pregnancy or the men who ask me if I make money in this field as a fat woman. In the United States, having a fat body—never mind having a fat body and being sexual—is an invitation for people to invade your emotional and physical space on a daily basis. I grew weary, fighting the day-to-day interactions, my own internal demons about my weight, and societal pressure as a whole. All the sexual empowerment that had been so hard won began to falter.

Then, impulsively, and at the suggestion of a man I was dating at the time, I moved to London, England. I figured: new country, new start. I began work as an admin for the marketing department of a well-known sports company. Forty hours a week to bring home less than I'd make for an hour of whippings and sex dissuaded me from "normal" work, and I quickly went back to my old ways, finding a flat to work out of, setting up some ads and a private phone number for work calls. And I waited.

The difference was obvious from the start. First of all, there was a sex worker union and message board I became part of, where the other members were queer, friendly, and welcoming. No one commented on my body, and many of the other members were fat ladies, too. It gave me confidence, and they gave me advice. Invigorated, I started to book clients, still a little nervous but willing to see if it was going to be different.

I thought I had found the Promised Land for fat hos.

The clients I had were polite and respectful, for the most part showing up on time, fresh, ready, and open-minded. Many of them, quite frankly, were attractive dorky guys I wanted to fuck anyway. My new clients adored my curves in a way San Francisco–types generally hadn't. They would lick my belly and kiss my thighs while I sighed dreamily at their British accents. Rather than overlook my body, they indulged in it, making me feel sensual on a level I didn't know was possible. And I didn't feel like I had to hide behind a euphemistic term, like *BBW*, anymore. I didn't even have to pretend to be straight or not a feminist. British clients seemed to like a sharp queer femme-inist who could match them intellectually and offer them a new outlook on sexual exploration.

That was just the tip of the iceberg. Dating in London was a world apart too. I found it easy to find lovers who found me as attractive as I did them and was surprised to find myself in demand. Telling people I was a sex worker mostly led to intelligent conversation, not ostrasization. After years of being forced into specialty shops with limited variety, going to shops on the high street and finding lingerie that fit me moved me to tears the first few times. I started being booked to perform at fetish/sex club events, something that was rare in the Bay Area for a fat chick. Even more surprisingly, I wasn't being booked as a tokenistic fat performer, but just as someone good at what she did. For the first time in my life, I felt like a person first, and a fatty second, and it felt amazing.

Now I'm back in the Bay with a British boyfriend, who thinks I'm the hottest thing alive and supports me in my work, and a sex working girlfriend who adores my curves. Even so, it's not always roses, despite having a lot more confidence under my sizable belt. Sometimes I panic that my one of my partners will leave me for someone else or that I'm not attractive enough to keep them. With my male partner, I worry that his attraction to my body stems from a fetishistic appreciation rather than a real love—though he's excellent at reassuring me. And with my female partner, because she's so conventionally gorgeous (slim and femme, with perfect skin), I compare myself to her, shocked when we're out and I get the attention instead of her. Sometimes, when it's dark and I'm looking over my bank statements, I freak out and wonder if I need to work out/ lose weight/get surgery just so that I can afford to hustle and continue to do this work full time rather than have a day job and fit it in part time.

Would I be happier with an average-size body? Logically, I know probably not. But the heart sometimes yearns for the body I *feel like* I have and the body I *actually* have to be the same. There's this anger at your body, a disassociation that happens. Why does the girl in the mirror not look like the girl I am in my mind?

Even though I'm very positive about my rolls and curves, I'm still very careful that the photos I put up to advertise my services show just the right angles. I make sure that my back rolls never or rarely show, that my underarms are well disguised, that my belly is looking round but smooth. And still, when I get naked, while I'm not as scared as I was, it's a *huge*, reassuring turn-on for my lover to pet or kiss my belly. I want my fat to be acknowledged and deemed sexy, not ignored or not mentioned. There's a political consciousness that comes about by being a fat, sexual woman. For me personally, I see my queerness and my fatness to be intertwined experiences in Othering. And sometimes that's exhausting, but I need to fight back against that little voice that asks me if I wouldn't be happier if I wasn't fat anymore, if I fit the "sexy" standard mold a little more easily.

But I'm not that kind of sex worker. People don't book me

if they're looking for a Porn Star Experience, all flowing hair and glossy lips. I see myself as a sexy fat queer sex worker and clients not into that can book elsewhere. I'm not in this for them. I'm in it for me. Sex work has taught me and continues to teach me valuable things about human sexuality, negotiation skills, and relationships, and I wouldn't want to give it up. And being fat has taught me a lot about human prejudice and how to stand up for myself.

Sex work can, of course, work both ways. There's nothing as crushing as putting up an ad for sexual services and finding that no one wants to buy. But I was startled by the way sex work made me feel good about myself because I was finding I was unable to keep up with the requests for appointments! There have been some moments with clients that have affected me and given me a confidence I didn't know I could have. One male client rested his head on my thick thigh, running his fingers along it and reverently whispering, "gorgeous, just gorgeous," and I glowed for a week. Another enjoyed watching—not just my breasts—but my belly and upper arms jiggle as he thrust into me, and his arousal fed my self-esteem.

And it's not just fat positivity that I receive either. I have enjoyed using my growing adoration of my fleshiness to raise the self-love of my clients as well. One woman I worked with, an older lady in her fifties who came to me with her husband, had not allowed him to undress her in years because she was self-conscious about what she called her "muffin top." Slowly, gently, my lips lightly on hers, I slid my hands under her shirt, not reaching for her breasts but for the softness of her belly's skin, stroking my fingertips over her and then bending to leave a trail of kisses. Watching her discover that not only did she not need to hide her body from me, but that I was aroused by it—that it could be an erogenous zone for her—had an intense effect on us both. A month later, I ran into them at a flea market, and she hugged me, tears in her eyes, saying that she felt sensual and at home in her body for the first time in thirty years.

Fat positivity can be personal revolution.

It can be political revolution as well, and often is. When the slut-shaming group, Porn WikiLeaks, was trying to get me to stop writing about their smear campaign, the worst thing they could think to say about me was that I was fat. It deflated them utterly when I shrugged and said, "Yeah, and?" It made me realize that it's impossible to shame someone who isn't ashamed of themselves. We need to stop letting guilt over our bodies be used as a weapon against us. This is a call to pudgy arms. Let's show our bellies and stop worrying if we have a fucking muffin top over our jeans or if our thighs bulge out of shorts. Let's throw away uncomfortable, chafing body-shaping tights and embrace sitting around naked. Let fatty become reclaimed and embraced in all its squishy huggable glory.

I am unapologetically a fat sex worker. And the gorgeousness of my fatness is not just a fetish; it's a reflection of the richness of who I am as a person and the sensual delights I have to offer . . . if you like what you see.

Dr. Strangelove, or How I Learned to Stop Worrying and Love My Fat

Jennifer Zarichnyj

Picture this: I am roughly twelve years old, most likely in a stretched-out Mets T-shirt (partly because I don't care, but mostly because I don't know any better) and fleece-lined sweat pants (see previous parenthetical aside), and I weigh 75 pounds more than most of my friends. It is a good thing that on this particular day in the sixth grade, a girl named Jessica told me that my pants made me look fat, because otherwise I would have been unaware. Humiliated, I sunk lower into my desk seat, covering my face with my unassuming, unstyled hair. Later that night, I would lock myself in my room and cry. I would forget to take off my glasses, which I had been wearing since the fourth grade. The lenses would be flecked with little white spots. If you have ever worn glasses while crying you understand this phenomenon.

This was not even the first time such a thing had happened. Once, we went swimming during gym class. I didn't have the best body, but I could get away with a bikini. In that chlorine-filled auditorium, I sauntered on over to the bleachers and took a seat next to the boy I had a crush on. He told me my stomach looked like his grandpa's and walked away. I was horrified. I was ugly.

At this tender age, I resented those who were smaller than me. Forget looking like the girl on the magazine cover; I just wanted to look like the girls in my class. Girls at the mall. Girls in my family. Any girl who didn't have to wear baggy clothes to hide her body. Sometimes, I would even think downright nasty thoughts. I'd see a skinny girl with an ugly face and feel like it was so unfair that someone like me, who had a nice face, got the short straw when it came to bodies and someone so unfortunate came out on top. I guess I was kind of a bitch.

It's not like I even ate anything that bad for me. I wasn't eating salad, but I wasn't gorging on McDonald's either. And since I was depressed all of the time anyway, I had no appetite. The concept of comfort food is bizarre to me. I guess I was just blessed with poor genes. I'd look at my mom; I'd take note of her shape: wide hips, big ass. My grandma was the same way. Together, they went to Weight Watchers meetings. They'd come home and flip through recipe books and count points, and they even bought a treadmill to work out on.

So eventually I joined them. My mom counted my points, and when I got home from school I walked on the treadmill. My motivation was that perfect body. I weighed myself every couple of days. I was not making much progress. I slipped deeper into depression. If a diet and exercise regimen didn't work, my options were becoming even more limited: liposuction, maybe an eating disorder, contracting some sort of disease.

In the meantime, I was counting down the days until I was out of grammar school forever. Everyone there obviously knew I was fat, and they did not let me forget it. I was looking forward to starting over in a school where maybe if my shirt was big enough and my hair covered enough of my face they would not notice I was fat.

I went to high school in another city. An all-girls school. No boys to feel awkward around. Perfect. I was nervous on that first day. My hair was still just a formless mop hanging out on my head, body still big, but I had a chance to start over with new people. I was brave for a little while. I was brave enough to make new friends and hang out with their guy friends. I was brave enough to smile and say "thanks" when we met new boys and they dated my friends and referred to me as "One of the Guys." It's okay; they weren't my type anyways.

Not that it mattered. My very first boyfriend, Dave, was an absolute mess. Everything I would never want in a boy. Short. Blond. Republican. He told those kinds of jokes that you laugh at to be polite but, secretly, you are embarrassed for the person telling them. We listened to Bruce Springsteen and Howard Stern in his car. I hated him, but he told me he loved me so I clung to him in desperation.

Five months and one hideous diamond necklace later, I called it quits with dear old Dave. I came to realize that being with him only made me feel worse about myself. I was quite obviously settling in every possible way, and the only reason why was because I was fat and, therefore, too ugly to date the boys I wanted to be with. After I broke up with Dave, I knew I needed a serious change, and if I couldn't lose weight I needed to try something else.

Just before I made the move to college, I cut off all my hair. I got layers. I flipped those layers out every morning with a curling iron. I hair-sprayed the hell out of each curl so it would hold all day. I felt a little better about myself, but slightly annoyed that I had to put so much more effort into how I looked because I was fatter than everyone else. When you are fat, you cannot take the easy way out. Otherwise, you become a statistic. At the time, I was just trying not to get made fun of anymore.

About two weeks into school, I got a Facebook message from a decent-enough-looking guy who told me I was cute. Looking at his profile, I noticed he had "fat girls" listed under his interests. I re-read it a few times, highlighting the text to make sure I wasn't imagining it. I felt very strange having this information presented to me. Part of me was severely offended. My whole life was spent trying to hide this blatantly obvious fact about myself. Was this guy messaging me because he noticed? The other part of me was convinced that it was a joke. This guy, Dan, was obviously trying to prank me. No one thinks fat girls are cute. No one thought I was cute.

We started talking, and it turned out that we actually had a fair amount of things in common—English majors with an ear for good music and pretentious enough taste in films ("Have you ever seen *Boondock Saints*?" "Blaaarghh!"). Occasionally, he'd slip in a reminder that I was attractive. He never once used the F-word though. He eventually started asking me if I'd want to meet up some time. I was too curious not to agree to hang out, and besides, I wasn't really used to this sort of attention.

My roommate, Amanda, who I had been friends with since high school, was there to witness my freak-out at the potential of Dating an Actual Cute Boy. Eyeing me up and down, she told me she "wasn't expecting me to meet someone so soon." At the time, I thought it was kind of a messed-up thing to say. Actually, I *still* think it's pretty messed up. Nonetheless, she helped me get ready for my first date.

I'll never forget it. Dan showed up at my dorm and, much like Amanda, eyed me up and down. But it was a very different kind of eyeing up and down. It made me feel a little excited. It also made me feel nauseous.

Standing next to him, I felt huge. He was the same height as me, but very tiny. Skinny arms, knobby knees. I was all flesh. I felt like I could break him just by looking at him. I was waiting for him to punch me on the shoulder and say, "Just kidding! I think fat girls are gross just like everyone else!" But he didn't. Instead, he sat on my bed and got comfortable. I gulped.

We sat around and watched *Ghost World*, except I wasn't really watching. I just kept on thinking to myself that there was a boy sitting next to me on my bed and he was cute and he was on my bed and sitting next to me. The movie ended without my realizing, and then he asked if I wanted to go for a walk. Even though boys didn't normally ask me to go for a walk with them, I knew this meant he was going to kiss me soon. I wanted to throw up. I said okay.

My head was essentially blank as we walked around the darkened campus. It was unusually cold for a September night, and I was wishing I had more on me than just a sweater. Dan wasn't wearing anything over his white Sleater-Kinney T-shirt. I silently wondered to myself if we were going to keep each other warm, wherever it was we ended up. I could tell he was looking for a secluded area, and we wound up under the stairs of Ben Shahn, a building I'd never been in. It was really dark under there, and I knew this was it.

He sat down. I sat down. We were Indian-style across from each other. He told me to move closer, so I did. I don't remember what happened next, but his face was really close to mine. And then his lips were on mine. I pulled away and felt my face flush to beet-red. "I've never done this before." I saw his jaw drop. He didn't say anything, so I apologized.

"You're a virgin?" The surprise in his voice was equivalent to that of a child finding where her parents hid the Christmas presents. I guess I mumbled a yes or something. I suppressed the need to laugh at the fact that someone could possibly see me as someone sexually active. Once he got over his shock, he asked if I wanted to try again. I said okay; at least now I'd made him aware that I was going to be bad at kissing.

Based on Dan's reaction, I had quite underestimated myself. For someone with no experience—aside from knowing how to get out of a car and act like it's nothing when someone tells you they love you—I was not doing half bad. So we kept kissing. And then Dan started doing something really weird. He started rubbing my belly. It felt pretty good, but I still felt awkward. It was, after all, the bane of my existence. When we eventually stopped kissing, he asked me what I thought.

"Well, it all felt pretty nice," I said. I was pretty flustered and probably stammering, but I can't remember.

"I meant what you thought of this," he said, touching my belly again.

"Uh, I dunno . . ." I trailed off. I felt like dying a little bit. Having to confront my body like this was torture. In that moment before he responded, I was completely embarrassed. I wished my fat wasn't so noticeable. I wished it wasn't something that needed to be discussed. And then:

"I like it. I like it a lot, actually." And then he kissed me again.

Dan walked me back to my room, and we saw each other pretty frequently until he eventually asked me out. In those first few weeks of dating, there were a lot of awkward fat-related moments. He told me that he was a Fat Admirer, or an FA for short. I confessed that I didn't know there were guys like that out there, and he laughed at me. I felt pretty silly.

I felt even sillier the first time he pulled me onto his lap. I squirmed to get up; I knew I would crush him. He looked at me like I had five heads, like I was speaking in tongues, when I told him I didn't want to hurt him. Without saying anything, he just patted his lap. I started to shake my head no, but he nodded. So I sat down very, very slowly. Clearly, my fat ass would not hurt him if I was moving at the pace of a snail. We sat like this for a while, watching *They Might Be Giants* on my laptop until I finally stood up and walked over to my bed and sat down.

"You aren't going to crush me, you know," he reassured me. I just shrugged and sat there until he came over to lie down with me.

Things were going fine up until our relationship made it to the next level: the level that would require me to be naked in front of him. It was the night after the Student Film Association's Hallow-een movie night, and we went back to his room. We were cuddling and eventually he started rubbing my belly—by now, I had become used to this and I actually really liked it. But then he went under my shirt, and I froze.

"You're so soft," and he moved down to kiss my belly.

He asked me if it was okay if he could see, and I hesitated. I knew what I looked like under that shirt. I knew that it was not the kind of belly that is allowed on the beach or even in a tight shirt. I knew that my belly had three rolls, and thinking about how it looked was making me feel very anxious in a very bad way.

As if he knew what I was thinking, he said, "It's not going to gross me out." So I took off my shirt.

He didn't say anything at first, but I saw his eyes light up. He started rubbing my belly, squeezing it, kneading it. Belly kisses were to become my favorite thing. It would be another week or so before I lost my virginity to him, but for the first time in my life I felt really desired, and it felt good. I had no idea that something that had caused me so much shame and grief could now make me so sexy in the eyes of someone else. And I liked that.

The way Dan looked at me when I was naked was almost better than the feeling of actually having sex. He appreciated me, every inch of me, and there were a lot of those. Once I got comfortable enough with him, I let him do silly things like jiggle me or blow raspberries on my belly. I can't imagine anyone else being able to relate to something like this unless you are fat and in a relationship with someone who loves it. I don't think blowing a raspberry on a set of washboard abs has the same effect.

Dan and I dated for two and a half years; our relationship was very flawed, but I'll save that for another time. However, I gained a lot from being with him, and I do not have any regrets that he was my first boyfriend. I'd be lying if I didn't say that he's the reason I can stand in front of the mirror after I get out of the shower without being totally repulsed. Sometimes when I'm talking to my mom, she asks me to tone it down because she says I'm "too conceited."

It's funny thinking about how awkward our first few dates were. I've started seeing another chub-lover, and he was the gauche one at first. My boyfriend, Matt, has always been attracted to bigger girls, but has never been in a relationship with one, let alone one as confident as me. When we first started dating, we were making out in his car and he "accidentally" felt me up. He stopped kissing me.

"I'm sorry! I thought that was your arm!" And then he looked embarrassed for wanting to squeeze my arm. And then he looked horrified, waiting for my reaction. And then we both started laughing. It's one of my favorite memories of him, right up there with another time when we were fooling around in his car and he asked me to get on top of him in the driver's seat.

"Uh, I dunno if I'll fit," I told him, eyeing the space between him and the steering wheel.

He said nothing, but reached down and pressed the button on the side of the seat to move it back and accommodate me. I still managed to honk the horn with my ass at some point. We're eagerly anticipating the release of *Fat Princess* for PlayStation 3 so we can play it together.

I'll probably sit on his lap while I play.

Inside Out

Tasha Fierce

I'm still in the process of actualizing the entirety of my inner ferocity.

I was first introduced to fat acceptance in 1998. I got my hands on a copy of the book *Fat!So?*. I was a newly minted adult and had also just decided to toss out my virginity. To accomplish this, I carefully picked someone I felt would be appreciative of getting laid at all, so I'd be assured it at least wouldn't be a *horrible* experience. Of course, I was happy when it actually turned out to be an incredible experience—and being the pleasure addict I am, I then wanted to do it *all the time*. But I'm not trying to talk about that right now. I'll get to the sex—but not details. This ain't erotica.

My mind was open to the possibilities of fat not being a complete social death sentence because of my recent "experience." *Fat!So?*'s message of living your life *now*, rather than waiting until you're some magic number on the scale, resonated with me. I was all about some instant gratification. Being the exhibitionist I am, I wrote all about my newfound love of fat and sex in my zine, *Bitch-core*, and online. And for a while things were good. I had a ton of sex, which is always awesome. Well, usually. There were some adventures. For my past self's sake, I wish I could say the body-hating bullshit ended there. But, as often happens, internalized fatphobia continued to fester inside me and slap me in the face occasionally—especially when it involved sex. Despite how I came to fat acceptance, I have a long, complicated, love-hate relationship with sexuality and being fat. That wasn't going to change just because I started fucking.

I had been what most average adults would call "chubby" (but what all *kids* would call "fat") for most of my elementary school years. In the beginning, the problem for me was just general teasing—the things all fat kids have to deal with. Because I'm half Black, I also dealt with teasing of the racist kind. But things didn't start getting really shady for me until I hit fourth grade and sprouted hips, tits, and an ass. General fat-kid teasing became sexual harassment and sometimes actual sexual assault. They had already made it clear that I was considered gross because I was fat. Somehow, though, they also now held the incompatible belief that my body was sexually desirable—and the cognitive dissonance that resulted made them angry at me.

This was definitely a *situation*. I quickly ascertained the parameters. So, my fat was inherently sexual when it was located at certain places—and at the same time hideous overall. I felt deep, psychic pain. Through the school's inaction and my wide-eyed belief in the words the boys said to me, I was taught that my body was a source of shame and that the way I looked was why these assaults happened. My body was why I was tormented, not because the school looked the other way and not because I had been taught to be too ashamed of myself to even tell my mother.

When I hit ninth grade, I decided to start wearing boy's clothes, stop wearing the little makeup I did, and draw as little attention to my over-sexualized body parts as I possibly could. I wanted to ensure that at least if I got shit for being fat, I wouldn't get harassed or assaulted. I wanted to be invisible. I felt I could make that happen by being completely nonsexual. I suppressed any attraction I had to anyone, period. I wanted to appear to guys as basically one of them. Being someone else was extremely appealing.

The depression that had set in when I began middle school became worse. I never dealt with the sexual assaults I experienced in elementary school through any kind of therapy. As you could imagine, my relationship with my body wasn't a healthy one. By May 1994, it had progressed to the point that I attempted suicide. I was hospitalized in an adolescent psychiatric unit, where I was eventually diagnosed with bipolar disorder and forced to take medication that ended up causing me to gain more weight—totally awesome when you're a teenager depressed about your body and dealing with trauma! Healthy environments, those psych wards. I really felt like they were promoting *healing*.

On the lighter side, the ward I was in was a co-ed unit, and I got to know a cute guy in there that was also labeled "crazy." Thinking back, he smelled damn good. I still make dudes wear Hugo. Smelling good is such a bonus, you know? Actually, it's a requirement. Anyway, he caused me to shed the guy shirts, and I started wearing tight, low-cut tops—but I kept the baggy guy jeans because I thought it made me look like a badass—whether or not it did is debatable.

The crazy guy was the first one I made out with, and I realized sometimes sexual/affectionate acts aren't dangerous or traumatizing. I liked it, so I decided to deliberately dress in provocative ways to attract the kind of attention I had previously avoided at all costs. This move was probably not completely based on healthy motives. Okay, in hindsight, it was obviously not based on healthy motives. But my unhealthy coping method ended up setting me down a path that at least landed me within twenty miles of the general vicinity of Loving Your Body Land. Of course, I battled with fat visibility and fat invisibility again many times later in my life.

From age fifteen until I left high school, my life was filled with mental breakdowns. Still, in between hospitalizations I managed to become the first fat cheerleader my school had seen, make flirting with football players a full-time job, get in *I'ma throw my box purse at you* fights with guys who harassed me, and skip school every chance I got. I was clearly a menace who had to be straightened out. So at sixteen, I was sent away to a long-term treatment facility. In the facility, my roommate introduced me to Bikini Kill, which in turn introduced me to the riot grrrl movement.

When I left treatment, I had revolutionary dreams and I was excited to get online to search out other girls who were interested in social justice. But at that point, I had no type of structure and nowhere to regularly go because I was out of school. I had already distanced myself from all my old friends. I began to isolate. The baggy clothes came back. I stopped caring about how I looked, or even if my clothes were clean. I became increasingly unsure of myself. Thought loops began to drive me crazy. I was convinced I'd never be in a relationship. I was convinced I was so ugly I was beyond hope. I decided to devote my time to activism and writing, because I figured a social life was out of the question. There was always that background noise when I left the house: *I'm worthless. I'm hideous. No one will ever be attracted to me.* I was accomplishing important things, but all I could think about was my fucking fat.

So now, we come full circle. At this point, I had to pull myself out of it. I put on clean clothes, combed my hair, and decided that I was ready to get laid. One of my friends sent me her used copy of *Fat!So?.* In short, MAGIC HAPPENED.

Naturally, I went on a manic sex spree. Soon *I* was suffering from cognitive dissonance. I now knew being fat wasn't bad, but the way I wanted to prove it to myself was to fuck guys like it was going out of style and hope one of them stuck around. I wanted a relationship, but my good night kiss was a blow job. Despite my best efforts, something good came out of it.

Near the end of my two-year fuckfest I met a very special boy online. We fell in love—before we had sex, before I even knew what he looked like. Literally. I saw his face for the first time when we finally met in person. We talked for hours every night for over a month. He decided to take the Greyhound from Oregon to Los Angeles to visit me for two weeks. A month afterward he came back to L.A. for good. I lived with him for a year before we got married. For nearly ten years, I didn't have to worry about sex and fat. I had someone who loved me for who I was, who thought I was beautiful and sexy and all that stuff we want a partner to think about us. I was incredibly spoiled, and when the ride came to an end, I found out I wasn't as confident about my body and as carefree about being fat as I thought I was. Damn rude awakenings.

Over the span of my marriage, I had ended up losing a lot of weight, some deliberately, some naturally. I was about a size 16/18 (from my high of size 28) when my husband left. I had just had my gallbladder removed because I developed gallstones during a two-year period of having hypothyroidism and going untreated (gotta love doctors who retire before they stop seeing patients). Before I had the surgery, I was being very careful about how much fat I ate, because high-fat meals trigger gallstone attacks. If you've never had the fun experience of thinking your life is ending—a gallstone attack—they can be excruciating. But after a while of careful eating, it had come to the point where *anything* I ate gave me attacks. So, on the run up to surgery I started eating high-fat food more often and just taking pain pills for the attacks. And after the surgery? Well, it was on as far as chicken and waffles were concerned.

My weight began creeping up. Stress eating, being free of gall-stone attacks, and leaving the house more often had me eating less than healthily. But I *just didn't care.* I was willing to take the blame, willing to shoulder the burden of my own fat. I was tired of repeating the excuses people had to give for being fat—*Oh, I exercise and eat well and I'm still fat! There's nothing I can do!* I wasn't exercising anymore. I wasn't eating well. And I didn't see why I had to justify my existence with good health. I didn't see why *anyone* should have to justify his or her existence with good health.

I was also starting to get out there and date—and I started having a lot of sex, date-related and otherwise. It felt good knowing I could be considered attractive by someone other than my husband again. And the fact that I was being considered attractive at a weight even higher than the one I'd been comfortable with emboldened me. I threw myself into pleasure, sexual and otherwise. I decided this was a sign that I should follow what made me happy, and if eating large quantities of fast food made me happy, then so be it. My room was often strewn with McDonald's wrappers, condoms, and sex-stained sheets. I embraced lust and gluttony. I reveled in sexual tension and the electric intensity of carnal desire.

Then suddenly, full stop. I realized it can't all be about people feeling good about having sex with me. What happens when the sex stops? What happens when you don't have a partner to tell you you're beautiful? How do you prepare for sex famine? These were questions I really had to answer, situations I would have to prepare for if I wanted to really love and understand myself. I had to learn to be the one to tell myself I'm beautiful. I also had to learn that external beauty isn't necessarily the ultimate goal. Subjectivity can't be a basis for an enduring positive self-image, it can only supplement one.

Sex became less of a central focus, and I channeled my energy into writing again. I expanded my subject matter from general social justice issues to sexuality and fat in particular. Beginning to write regularly about the two allowed me to examine my own beliefs and uncover biases I had yet to confront. It strengthened my self-image and helped me solidify in my mind what I wanted in a partner—and what I could offer *to* a partner—which was invaluable work. Writing is really how I've come to understand myself. I still try to write down my thoughts as much as I can every day.

I feel like I'm telling this story as if it has an ending. It doesn't really. Loving yourself is a journey that ain't got a destination. Over a year has passed since the furor of my newly single, hedonistic days. I have grown and changed in incredible ways over that time. I'm having less sex, but it's somewhat by choice. I eat healthier now, but I eat healthier because I want to support my mental quality of life, not because I'm trying to claim innocence. I still think it's important to be willing to accept fatness by choice. Because sometimes it is a choice—and there's absolutely nothing wrong with that. Yet you can't love yourself if you don't embrace the choices you've made to become who you are. I learned that along the way, too.

As an ending to this story with no end, I want to make sure that you know that it's okay to not be perfect at being fat or loving your body. It's okay to be nervous about taking off your clothes in front of a guy. It's okay if you're worried that a new sex partner is turned off by your body. No one is brave and fierce *all* the time. So many young women have expressed these fears and others like them to me in shame, as if it's breaking the rules to have insecurities. Our society puts a lot of importance on "strength." We who have been at this for a while often don't share when something bothers us. I think that gives a lot of people—especially people new to the fat acceptance movement—the idea that at some point you're beyond all the bullshit. It gets easier, definitely. But there are going to be times when it's *really fucking hard*.

If you learn anything from my story, I hope it's this: you deserve to love yourself. You deserve sexual pleasure. You deserve someone who loves you and who loves your body as much as you do. You *can* overcome years of conditioning. And you *will* get there. You will survive, and eventually, you will thrive.

Pecan Pie, Sex, and Other Revolutionary Things

Virgie Tovar

I am one of those progressive, fat-loving, fat-activist fat girls. I'm one of those whoopie-pie-in-one-hand-vibrator-in-the-other kind of fat girls. I'm one of those take-no-prisoners, potty-mouthed, kiss-my-ass, guerilla fatties, and my weapons of choice are pink, glitter, cleavage, and impossibly short dresses.

And, no, I'm not sorry.

People often want to know how exactly a fat, brown girl manages to learn to love a body that is perpetually under attack. Well, falling in love with my body took a long time. Like any good love story, there was drama and tears, false starts and heartbreak, pecan pie binges and dirty sex.

In the beginning, I was born under a funny star. My grandmother says that the angels went through the entire baby Bloomingdales in heaven just to find me. Some of the babies were too light-skinned to be a half-Mexican half-Iranian baby, and some had freckles, which no one in the family had. Some were too skinny, and some didn't have any hair on their heads. By the time my mother was on the delivery table—screaming and hurling epithets—my fate had been determined. The angels had chosen a little fat girl with curly black hair, a penchant for sweet things, and a tendency toward sexual precociousness.

My mom was twenty and about 350 pounds then. She loved sewing lace onto mini-skirts, staying out all night, and filching small beads, tweezers, and anything too small or cute to resist (to this day whenever we go out she offers to get me anything I want as long as it's roughly the proportions of a human hand). Before I was born, she ate a lot of fish. She read an article about the importance of Omega-3 fatty acids in fetal brain development and ate as much fish as she could get her hands on: anchovies, tuna, shrimp (lots of shrimp). Right up until Mom was ready to burst, she worked at the mecca of West Coast chocolate boutiques: See's Candies. She tells me of the Olympic-size pizzas (Olympic size is the size that's after extra large) and the pound of chocolate she stole from work every day—a new flavor for every day of the month, from milk chocolate caramel chews to marshmallow-dipped nuts and toffee. My father wasn't really around, but he was a skinny Iranian international student at the community college that my mom went to. He loved money, large stacks of books, and really tight bell bottoms. He also had a reputedly hard time sharing food with others.

Imagine four fat Mexicans and one chubby little half-Mexican driving to get Chinese take-out in a 1979 Pinto, and you've got the day after my birth. My grandma says that I slept peacefully for the time I was in the hospital, but the moment I smelled that *mushu*, I was awake and ready to fulfill my destiny. As a little girl, I was self-assured and had an affinity for flirtation and sweet-and-sour pork. I liked dressing up and masturbation. I'm not sure how I figured out how to masturbate, but I thought I was the only person in the world who knew it existed and spent many an evening planning out how I would make my fortune by training people to do it to other people for a lot of money. I called it "vagina tickling," and I can't imagine how I knew that my hoo-haw was called a vagina, but I didn't know the word for masturbation.

I was hot shit in preschool. I had an uber-hot Chinese boyfriend named Ray-Ray, and he loved me for my body. Ray-Ray was about half my size, and every day after school I remember feeling my heart beating quickly, pumping blood into my cheeks. I could hear it loudly in my ears. I would lie spread out completely—like a little olive-toned, pot-bellied snow angel—on the big rug that had all the alphabet letters and the numbers 0 through 10 embroidered into it. And I would wait for Ray-Ray to run from the edge of the rug and fall on top of me, hugging me, laughing with me, loving me.

The age of five proved to be the year of my inauguration into a world where my fat wasn't hot anymore. I lost my sense of self when I was introduced to the evil, dark, and horrible world of primary school. I realized recently—while completing my master's thesis on fat women and femininity—that my perception of myself as a girly girl changed around the age of five when I began being made fun of every single day. The taunting attacked my body, the temple of my femininity. I distinctly recall not feeling like a girl. I didn't feel like a boy, simply an un-girl. When I was in fourth grade, I had a best friend named Lorna. She was very petite, and every day during lunch we would enact a romance that we'd read about in a very popular series of novels for pre-teens, *The Baby-Sitters Club*. Though we did not discuss it, it was tacitly understood that I would play the boy. I always played the boy, and even though I desperately yearned to play Mary Anne, I knew that the request was impossible. The girl could never be as big as I was.

The crushes I had were violently unrequited. So, I simply learned to stop having them. I tried to ignore the kids who teased me, but they were *surprisingly* not to be deterred. (It turns out that telling fat children to ignore bullies is placing the blame of verbal abuse onto the fat kid, reinforcing psychologically that they must bear the onus of the behavior; I wish I'd been advised to snitch to my heart's content.) I tried to diet, but that usually didn't last more than a few days. So, by the time I was fifteen, I had immersed myself fully into pastimes more suitable for social outcasts: the marching band, the debate team, church, and the Junior Classical League, the club for fat, acne-ridden, college-bound high-schoolers who love the language of ancient Rome: Latin.

Sometimes after school my mom would take me to what we called simply "the canned food store," which is like the Ross for food (everything was "slightly irregular"): the last stop, the food morgue. When enormous cans of peaches got dented, they got sent to the canned food store. When a huge batch of chocolates was wrapped with the wrong wrapper, it was sent to the canned food store. And sometimes you had to guess what might be wrong with the food because there were no visible signs of irregularity. But they took food stamps, and we had those.

The canned food store had the best pecan pies in the whole world. I've always had a love of pastries, and it doesn't get much better than some good-ass pecan pie. My mom loved pecan pie, too. She never quite knew how to deal with the anguish that my fat caused me as a child, but she always had a new tip on how to finally beat it. These were all ideas she'd tried on herself first, I could tell. That day we made a trip to the canned food store because I had been made fun of (for the 1,005th day in a row) and was inconsolable.

She said that a sure way to lose weight was to learn to hate the food that tasted the best because that was the food that made you fat. She said we could get one pecan pie each, eat the whole thing until we were sick and then the idea of pecan pie would never appeal to us again, therefore, crossing it off the list, ready to move onto the next sinful item. I can still remember how good that pecan pie was and how I knew—in my little, subversive heart—that I could never give up pecan pie. I didn't finish the pie or get sick, but I guess this set the stage for more experiments.

Puberty in my grandparents' conservative, religious, Mexican household was hard on my burgeoning sexuality. I refer to that era as "Pussy Lockdown." I wasn't allowed to date or go out alone; walking to the mailbox on the corner was pushing it. I was not taught to ride a bicycle or skate, nor was I allowed near a trampoline or a car lest I attempt to escape and, what, suck every dick in the neighborhood? I'm not sure what exactly they were afraid of. Okay, I guess if I were to be honest, I was a girl whose future slut potential was apparent in the way that I batted my eyes at my cousins, the cashier at the grocery store, the pastor of our church, or really anyone who looked like a boy. But I was a Sunday School teacher too, and when I wasn't teaching toddlers about hell or learning how to conjugate Latin verbs, I was masturbating. By the time I was eighteen, my hormones were ready to have a debutante ball all their own. My young adulthood was just about to begin; it would prove to be the point in my story where those punk-ass suburban kids got proven wrong, the point in my story where I would discover my delicious sexuality anew—and how my round, chubby body was every bit a part of that deliciousness.

Once I officially became a grown-up, I found the love for myself that I'd lost so many years before. I attribute some of the self-love rediscovery to the part of my brain that knew that something just wasn't right with a world that told me that I had to wake up every morning to the fascistic sound of an alarm clock, a world that said I had to exercise and eat carrots, a world that said that ice cream was bad.

Some of the self-love came from the men I dated who told me I was hot, sexy, and beautiful in addition to being interesting, smart, and funny. When I walked into my femininity, I was inundated with fat love from men. Some of them were researchers, waiters, lawyers, inventors, bus boys, salesmen, security guards, grad students, accountants, financial advisors, computer programmers, the guy who sells cable car tickets in San Francisco, executive directors of nonprofits, natural history experts, nurses, geneticists, professors, high-school vice principals, and Facebook employees. Some were married, rich, blind, twenty-ish, forty-ish, vegetarians, submissives, pathological liars, Republicans. Some of the men seemed simply pleased to be with me, but most of them were really quite overjoyed. Some of them loved me, some of them didn't, but they helped me to remember that deliciously erotic part of me, the part I'd thought I'd lost.

Everything I experienced sexually and romantically was against everything that *Cosmopolitan* or Ab Roller ads had told me about life all those years. If my body wasn't hot, then why did men want me to model lingerie? Why did they take me shopping and to fancy restaurants? Why did they want to squeeze my fat during foreplay? Why did they want to kiss my belly, suck my toes, ask me to jiggle my boobs in their face or, even more baffling, sit on their face? Why did these men buy me presents or ask me to tie them up or call them dirty names? I thought that's not what people are supposed to want to do with 230-pound women. But here I was getting my ass eaten and being thanked for the privilege!

Then I got into the University of California, Berkeley. Berkeley had been a distant memory from my childhood. My grandfather occasionally drove the fifteen miles from our house to Berkeley to show me how wild Berkeley people were. They were the people who stood at the far end of revolutionary politics. He said there were hairy ladies who slept with other ladies, who didn't think men were so important. He said there were people who had casual sex and smoked marijuana and sometimes didn't wear clothes when they left the house. Well, my grandfather was right!

While attending UC Berkeley, I met a bunch of brilliant, cerebral, radical feminists who taught me my first real lessons in body love. We talked about our feelings. We cried and thought. We wrote in journals. They taught me how to think critically about the messages that our world sends to women. They mostly taught me that in a society like ours, women are taught to live for men, and not for themselves. They thought that was a load of horse shit. They had hair under their armpits and on their legs. We burped and farted and made smoothies with fruit we'd gotten out of dumpsters. They encouraged me to be as fat and perverted as I wanted to be and also to become a lesbian, but I just wasn't that into pussy. They were beautiful.

At twenty, I became a phone sex operator and learned how to talk about desires and fantasies. I learned from my clients that sexuality is infinitely complicated and remarkably malleable. I started learning how to talk about my fat in an erotic way and encouraged my partners to tell me about how sexy they thought my fat was. And they did! I learned that a lot of men liked my fat a lot.

I started to become excited about the idea of being a radical fat girl. And one day, when a woman on the commuter train told her boyfriend in a loud whisper that I was too fat to wear the very fabulous outfit I had on, I gave her a big slice of bitch pie. I walked right up to her—my face no more than a foot from hers—and told her that my body was mine, that I could wear whatever I wanted to wear, that she needn't be threatened by my short skirt, *and* that I looked good, *real* good. I did not insult her or berate her. I simply felt it polite to inform her that the era of fat-girl apologies and tastelessly retrograde fatphobic remarks is coming to a close and the day of the fierce, too-much-to-handle fat girl is close at hand. And then I sat down . . . right next to her. We sat there in silence for forty-five minutes, from downtown San Francisco all the way to the Pacific Ocean, the end of the line. I felt like the Rosa Parks of fat that day.

A fierce fat girl knows her fat is political, that her fat says "fuck you" to the rules, that her fat is all hers, and that she ain't takin' shit from no one. I've decided that I am going to love my body come rain or shine, through the boy droughts and the man rivers, through the days when I want to wear my big, ugly mint-green night gown and the days when I want to wear my cheetah-print platform heels. I've decided that the world is a strange and arbitrary place. But it's also a place filled with flowers and chocolate and cheese. And a world filled with these things isn't hopeless.

What we forget is that pleasure is our right as people. And pleasure is provided by delicious food, good sex, sleeping in, masturbating, scratching mosquito bites, wearing panties with cherries on them, licking the cake spoon, loving with abandon, petting puppies, cups of hot chocolate, jokes about Jesus's obvious homosexuality, big tacky jewelry, and magically finding one more cookie at the bottom of the Pepperidge Farms package.

Fatties are the vanguards of pleasure. We flout convention and become the models of corporeal anarchy. Some folks love anarchy, others find it distasteful, and still others find it threatening. Empowered fatties are living renegades against the rules. The rules dictate that we girlies should all fall in line; wear only black, gray, or brown; not show cleavage; and not take up too much space.

But I know a different life. I know a life where wardrobes are full of pinks and oranges, where fatties wear bright red flowers in their hair, where shoes are optional, and glorious mouths open while big tummies rollick when women laugh.

It's called the Cook Islands.

The Cook Islands are in the middle of the Pacific Ocean, the closest thing to paradise on Earth. I visited the capital of the Islands, Rarotonga, in 2009. This is a magical place, where giant clams stake their place on the lagoon floors, where glow worms dance during full moons, where a 700-year-old language still percusses on the tongues of every inhabitant, where papaya is perfected by humidity and sunlight, and where the dragonflies are as big as hummingbirds.

There's only one road that circumnavigates Raro, and lagoons are never more than ten feet away. You can touch electric blue starfish just below the water's surface while bright yellow fish scuttle past your toes. You can pick star fruit, mangoes, and coconuts from trees beside the road. Television is comprised of one channel. Dishes are made up of coconut milk and lime, raw fish and spinach, and chicken cooked in an underground oven called *umu*. Here you wear a flower behind your left ear if you're taken and behind your right ear if you're single. This island is green and lush. And the women are huge. Well, pretty much everyone is.

When I got off the plane, the tourists from New Zealand, Australia, and Europe looked emaciated next to the Cook Islanders. I felt so at home with my dark hair, my brown skin, and my big, fabulous self. In the Pacific, my body is normal. Big arms don't hide behind cardigans. Women wear sarongs and sandals. They have big breasts and big asses and big thighs. Here women eat because their food is delicious, and healthy doesn't mean carb-free.

On Sunday, people go to church. I had read about the high fashion of Cook Island church ladies in a guide book and decided that for the first time in a long time that there was something at a church that was worth seeing. I was walking from my guesthouse to the church when I got picked up by a couple in their little Honda. They said they "had a feeling" I was headed to their church. The women wore gorgeous white dresses and enormous hats. After the service at the Cook Islands Christian Church, some of the church ladies set up a table and everyone was welcome to eat homemade donuts and crumpets smothered charitably with butter and jam, breadfruit and paw paw, ginger snaps and juice. Everything was so good, and eating was an event that brought people together over a shared experience of delight.

The Cook Islands really messed with my worldview. Before visiting the Pacific, I had never been to a place where big wasn't bad, where big was normal. I had never been to a place where big, fat, beautiful women walked arm in arm, smiling and sharing secrets. It turned everything I had accepted as "just the way things are" on their head. It reminded me that fat life doesn't have to be what it is out there. And that sometimes all it takes is a flower in your hair and a secret in your heart to change the way the world looks.

There are other important parts and players in my story that seem to have no neat place, but somewhere during all those years, I became a lot of things and loved a lot of people. In the years since the Cook Islands, I've become a burlesque performer, a fat activist, and a fat studies scholar.

I've learned about the power of my fat from a lot of people. I've learned that it makes some people happy and others mad, some horny and others critical, some comfortable and others ill-at-ease. I've learned that sometimes I inspire other women just by talking about my fat-girl sexuality and wearing tight clothes. I've learned that every fat girl I've met has a pretty interesting sex life. And I've learned that my body is yummy, and that loving it is far more fun than not loving it. Like real love, I've got to fight to keep it. Like real love, I've got to believe I deserve it. Like real love, I mess up over and over, but I forgive myself and I try not to make the same mistakes again.

When you're a fatty, eating a cupcake in public is a radical act. When you're a fatty, wearing a short skirt or a tight dress is revolutionary. When you live in this world, loving your round, flabby body is avant-garde. We're the coolest people we know.

Self-love is a minute-to-minute entity. It never stops being hard to love yourself in a world that tells you that you'll never be good enough. Self-love will not save you from getting your heart broken (in fact, it will make things riskier). But no act of love (especially self-love) will ever be a wasted effort. Being a fabulous fat girl is not easy. It may be the hardest thing one ever decides to be. I am criticized. I am chastised for my role in spitting on the shiny, brown loafer of "the man." People are jealous and passive aggressive. They whisper. They haterade.

But I strut my ass through the world with the knowledge that no one can touch the secret part of me that knows I'm a queen.

PART 3

FASHION

Fashion is about more than cute open-toed shoes, gold leather clutches, or amazing leopard-print tights (although, even if it weren't about more than that I'd be pretty happy with some leopard-print tights). Fashion has so much to do with freedom and visibility: the freedom to wear things that make us feel good and the visibility that comes with polka dots, sequins, and the occasional bow tie. Fashion is art, style, and play. Fashion—or Fatshion—has inspired fat girls to take to the blogosphere and the runway. Fat-girl clothing swaps and fat-girl flea markets create opportunities to strip down, put on something hot, and allow other fat girls to fawn over how well you're "working" that look. Independent plus-size designers—like Jeannie Ferguson of Big Girls United, Monif Clarke of Monif C, Jasmine Elder of

Jibri, Tracey Broxterman at Domino Dollhouse, Bertha Pearl at Size Queen Clothing, Tenille McMillan from NakiMuli, Rachel Kacenjar at Sweettooth Couture, and Gisela Ramirez—create incredible pieces for big bodies.

In this section, you will read about fashion tips and tricks, the way that a single garment can change a life and, of course, you will read gratuitous Fatshion talk.

Oh yes, this revolution will be accessorized, altered, and adorned with faux fur.

Blue Pants

Jessica Judd

Deafened by screams of approval and thunderous applause, I pull myself out of my final pose, a backbend over my prop chair, and catch the eye of a fellow dancer as she flashes me a smile worth a million bucks. Our fat dance troupe, the Phat Fly Girls, has just nailed our fat-positive version of "Mein Herr" (yes, that one, from *Cabaret*), and the crowd is going wild. Squeezing seven fat dancers wearing little more than fancy undergarments onto a tiny bar stage, we just showed what it means to represent for fierce fatties.

We do this a lot. Hell, I've been doing it for ten years, as long as the Phat Fly Girls have existed. In that moment and all those like them, I feel everything fabulous, empowering, and downright fierce that we are as a troupe of fat dancers and that I am as a self-loving fat woman making my way through this fat-hating world. But I know we, the fierce fat ones, are not even supposed to *be*. I am not supposed to be able to do a backbend over a chair, and I certainly am not supposed be doing it to widespread audience approval in a body-revealing costume flanked by other scantily clad fatties onstage. That's not the story we've been sold, but it's the one we're living. David Byrne, forever in my head, I think, "Well, how did I get here?"

It all started with a pair of blue pants.

Well, it didn't exactly start there, but a particular pair of blue pants holds an uncanny significance for me. They mark a crossroads of sorts, the point at which I started down the path I am on, the one that led me to slowly realize that I was not just temporarily fat, that my fatness was not a passing phase, that I wasn't just a dancer who happened to be fat, but that I was a bona fide fat dancer, and that I'd better find a way to make some peace with that or I'd never be truly happy.

That was a lot.

Let's start from the top . . .

. . . 5, 6, 7, 8.

I wasn't always a fierce fat dancer. I wasn't always a dancer, and I wasn't always fat. I have probably always been a little bit fierce. Like so many little kids across the United States, I started dance lessons when I was young, around five. I loved it and was good at it. I was one of those kids onstage who was always smiling, who knew all the moves, and who kept dancing and smiling through epic costume or prop failures like the time my balloon popped prematurely during the Balloon Ballet. During my early dance years, I was firmly on the thin side of average. My size was never a cause for concern from dance teachers, no cause for whispers, no cause for anyone to think I didn't belong based on my body's size and shape.

While I enjoyed dance, when I was about ten I felt it was time to move on to other pursuits like competitive athletics where I expended my considerable physical energy throughout junior high and high school. During this time, I would have passing fantasies of dancing again as I was a frequent audience member at my younger sister's dance recitals. I wanted to dance but was afraid to largely because I was convinced that despite my small size I had become too fat to dance. The costumes, they terrified me. What if I took a class and then the teacher ordered a midriff-baring costume for the recital? What would I do? The horror!

While it sounds kind of funny to my fierce fabulous fatty self twenty-plus years later, I still have a whole lot of empathy and sympathy for the me that feared showing the world my bare stomach. And it wasn't just the stomach. I feared the shimmer tights (okay, those are arguably universally terrible, just because) and tight spandex dance pants. I couldn't stand the thought of getting up onstage wearing such things for all the world, and my high-school peers, to see.

So, I didn't dance. I thought about it, but I didn't do it. I took aerobics instead: a sad, cheap stand-in for an actual dance class. There I at least got to do choreographed movement even though it was typically mind-numbingly boring and done to bad music and involved a lot of talk of fat burning, pulse rates, and feelin' the burn.

As I got older, despite all the aerobics classes, and partly due to chronic dieting and disordered eating, I got bigger. I started to get precariously close to becoming an actual fat person. Like, my clothing size crossed over into the *double digits*. There were years of anguish around this, resulting in more disordered eating and exercise patterns and shame, and . . . you get the picture.

Fast-forward to the spring of 1998. I was twenty-three and in graduate school and needed two more units in my class schedule to get my financial aid. I had completed or was already enrolled in all my required coursework so I searched for something fun, and Jazz Dance II caught my eye. Somewhere, the larval fierce fatty inside me said, "Go for it," and I did. I was bigger than I had ever been, and I knew fat people weren't supposed to dance, but I decided to do it. No shame, no regrets.

If you are keeping track, you will observe that it had been roughly thirteen years since I had last taken a real dance class so it should be of no surprise to learn that the class kicked my fat ass.

Through all my struggles and heartbreak with double pirouettes and floor work that semester, something came alive inside me—something that said, "Keep dancing."

I did. I started taking jazz, tap, hip-hop, and lyrical classes at a local private studio. I worked hard, really hard. I was older than the majority of students at the studio and always the fattest. I knew this, but I kept showing up even though I got the distinct feeling that no one would ever take me truly seriously as a performing artist at my size. I also had a small secret I carried with me. I wanted to perform in the studio's annual dance recitals, and I vowed to myself that I would regardless of the costumes and how I felt I looked in them. I held this inside, and it often kept me going, a tiny act of fat pride, even if I didn't know quite how to conceptualize it yet. I believed it was important to honor myself enough to be in the shows, to not hide and pretend like I wasn't really in the class and that it was monumentally important for fellow students and audience members to see a real, live fat person onstage.

Baby steps to fat liberation. Baby steps.

I did this for the better part of three years with no real issues. Then the blue pants happened.

Recital time had come, and costumes were purchased for my hip-hop classes, only they weren't ordered out of a dance costume catalog wherein spandex is king. Instead someone had gone to a department store and purchased street clothes for our costumes—from the juniors department.

You heard me, from the juniors department.

As many of us learned when we were about ten, the juniors department houses clothing appropriate only for a very small range of sizes and for an even smaller range of body shapes. My "misses" size 14/16 ass hadn't seen the inside of a juniors department in *years*. To my utter horror, I was handed a pair of blue pants to try on, a size thirteen 100-percent-cotton-so-they-won't-stretch pair of pants, pants that I knew I was not going to fit into. My well-meaning but deluded classmates kept telling me they "ran big" and

I should just try them on. I sucked it up, went to the changing area, gave it a shot, and encountered the inevitable inability to pull the pants over my hips. Collecting myself, I walked the pants calmly back and explained they did not fit and started to warm up with the rest of the class thinking I could shake it off. Then I felt the tears coming as my face got hot. I was mortified. I was embarrassed, ashamed, and hurt. For the first time, I really felt at my core the essential way in which I was different than everyone else in my class and how that difference was not being honored. I was fat and as a result not really a dancer.

I spent days being upset. I cried, I moped, and finally I found comparable blue pants in my size to use for my costume. I danced in my own larger-than-a-size-thirteen blue pants and tried to not feel shame about it. No one could tell from the audience that I had on different pants than the rest of the class, but I knew. I knew I needed the fat pants.

It gave me pause. After the shame and sadness came anger—anger that my body and I were not considered in the costume-purchasing process and anger that this was made to be my problem. The anger started me down the road to fierce fatness and led me to a place that would become transformative for me and thousands of others.

Fortuitously, a couple of months prior to attempting to squeeze my ass into the blue pants, I had gone to the first ever Bodies in Motion concert, an all-fat dance concert produced by the newly formed Big Moves, a service organization dedicated to promoting size diversity in the world of dance. The founder of Big Moves, Marina Wolf Ahmad, chatted me up at the ticket table and was interested in my dance background.

I was moved by her introduction to the show, done in her signature red tutu. She asked, "Is this too much?" and went on to explain, through barely held-back tears how as fat people, as fat dancers, we are "too much." It resonated. I felt it, and while I found the show interesting, I was conflicted about the thought of being a part of any sort of all-fat dance company. I was still laboring under the delusion that my fatness was inconsequential, apolitical, and wholly personal in terms of dance. I was still happy to try to pass and thought that I could someday be thin enough to look like other dancers. Despite my uncertainty, when Marina contacted me several months later asking me to join the Big Moves advisory board I figured I'd give it a go. It was the fall of 2001, and my life has since changed in ways I could not have imagined.

Joining the Big Moves advisory board meant I was immediately rubbing elbows and brainstorming with some serious fat activists. In addition to Marina, I was now working with *Fat!So?*'s Marilynn Wann and Carol Squires of FAT LIP Readers Theater. I was schooled in fat liberation, fat activism, and body positivity in a sort of fat-immersion program. I was ready for it. I stopped dieting and started to work on ways to truly love my body as it was, appreciating it for its beauty and for everything it could do.

At the time, I also started taking Marina's size-positive hip-hop class. After one or two classes, she roped a few of us into cobbling together a performance ensemble to be called the Phat Fly Girls and we, after not much rehearsal, already had a gig at a BBW dance party.

I still remember the night of the dance party, how foreign and familiar it all was. Familiar because performing a dance in front of an audience was nothing new to me. Foreign because that night was the first time in my adult performing life that I felt absolutely, 100 percent fucking awesome and fabulous walking out to perform. I was surrounded by body positivity and support, which utterly transformed how I saw myself in that moment. It was the first time I was not only unself-conscious about my costume, but that I was also feeling downright fierce, sexy, and beautiful in a costume. It was positively amazing to perform for people who were genuinely excited about seeing fat dancers. I started to think that I deserved more than to be merely tolerated as a fat dancer, which was how I felt the mainstream dance world treated me . . . with tolerance.

I saw tiny glimpses of what power could be held by groups of fat people performing. Our ragtag little group owned it that night, and that is how the Phat Fly Girls and my actualization as a fierce fatty began. I had a taste and I wanted more.

That night marked the beginning of my performing career with Big Moves. I have spent many years with the Phat Fly Girls, first as a dancer and since 2008 as co-artistic director and a choreographer. For five years, I managed and danced in Big Moves' now-defunct modern dance company, Mass Movement, and was administratively involved with Big Moves until 2009, serving as director of Big Moves Bay Area from 2004 to 2009, and as a board member from 2001 to 2004. Big Moves is my home, my family, my people.

As a fat dancer with Big Moves, I have performed everywhere from the Great American Music Hall to funky dive bars cum hipster hangouts. I have performed in university theaters, underground (literally) theaters, as part of an art installation, and alongside a presentation about biodiesel. I've danced at fat events and nonfat events. I've danced for audiences who knew what to expect and audiences who really didn't seem to know what hit them. I've been on *Entertainment Tonight*, PBS, CurrentTV, local news, radio shows, and in photo essays. That's a long way from crying over not fitting into a pair of blue pants.

Through all those performances, big, small, awesome, and awesomely weird, I have gained an appreciation for the importance of being a fat dancer and the importance of fat dance troupes. I used to think being the lone fatty onstage was enough. I thought that my presence in a mainstream studio would be enough to bring fatties into the dance world. I was wrong. When we are the token fatty onstage, we are easy to dismiss. We are an anomaly, the random fatty who can dance. We are viewed as mostly inoffensive, as just one freak mixed in with a bunch of "real" dancers. We can be tolerated often because we are presumed to be working toward the holy grail of thinness. When the Phat Fly Girls take the stage, and there are six, seven, eight, or more of us, all unapologetically fat, all dancers, our existence cannot be denied. We are no longer an anomaly. We cannot be explained away as exceptions. We demand to be taken seriously as fat people and fat performers who are not trying to become unfat. We are fierce.

As the Phat Fly Girls have grown from a scrappy troupe to the more polished, skilled, and coherent performing company we are today, we continually push the envelope with our costume choices. Dressing in caftans we are not. We love our shiny, bedazzled, body-revealing costumes. We don't wear black for its slimming effect. We work that shiny turquoise, pink leopard print, and gold lamé. We wear ruffle-butt panties for pants and bras with adornments for tops. This is nothing new for the average dancer, but for fat dancers, it is downright revolutionary.

Of course, it's not just about the costumes. It is about the attitude, the self-love, the acceptance, and the liberation that comes from living a fierce fat life. No one can take that away from me. When I get up on that stage and I work it, and I sell it, and I dance it the best I possibly can and then some, I am living my dream. Creating art and being expressive in an outlaw body, in a body that is not supposed to be creating art of this kind, is an act of revolution. It took me a while to fully understand the effect of what the other dancers and I were doing, but I see it now. I dance with the Phat Fly Girls because I love dancing, I love performing, and I am happiest doing it in a place where my body is truly free. I also do it because it is damned important work. People need to see fat people dancing somewhere other than weight-loss reality TV shows. When we dance, when we lift each other, when we pirouette, leap, and do the splits to the floor we challenge everything our society has been told fat people can and cannot do. I force people to look at me and see me. When I am onstage in a shiny dance dress, my fat has nowhere to hide. I don't apologize for it. It is me. My fat body can do some really amazing things. I am not going to hide it, onstage or otherwise.

I never expected that this was where dance would take me. I had long assumed that the most I could hope for was annual recitals at a studio, and maybe, just maybe, a spot in a dance company who deigned to tolerate my body nonconformity. I never dreamed of the opportunities I've had since becoming a fierce fat dancer.

Clearly, the blue pants didn't start all this. I learned to dance and perform long before I was fat and long before I was asked to wear pants that would only fit a Barbie-size version of me. I was fat and thinking about what that meant some time before I ever saw those blue pants. But those pants . . . they changed something. They signified a crossroads where I had to choose a path, and I chose the one I couldn't see clearly, the one with countless twists and turns. Through dance and performance with Big Moves, I started and continued down that path, a path with hidden pots of gold manifested in the form of fierce fat liberation, a prize I didn't know existed until I was holding it and one I treasure every day.

On Dressing Up:
A Story of Fatshion Resistance

Kirsty Fife

'm fat.

I weigh around 18 stone/260 pounds, though I weigh myself rarely. I'm 5'9" tall, and my measurements are about 47-42-52, though these vary also. I generally fit a UK size 22 or 24, and I have large, wide, size-8 feet. I am a definite pear shape, with a big belly that people often assume contains a baby (nope, just a lot of good food and drink). I have hips that don't fit through doors, in seats, or in the majority of mass-produced clothes. I've always been fatter than most of the people in my immediate social circles, and that fatness is something that I've been in constant negotiations with. There are spaces that my fat body makes it impossible to be in, and that's something that used to make me angry at myself. I'm lucky that now this anger is something I'm able to channel toward the external sources that exclude and alienate my body, instead of internalizing it toward my own body.

Fashion has always been a huge part of my life, and it is through clothes that I began to accept my body. Clothes have been a passion of mine since I was a teenager. I grew up in a relatively poor family, and we often couldn't afford to buy new clothes. Instead, my dad and I would hit the local charity shops (and growing up in a small suburb, there were many!), scouring the £1 racks for hidden gems. I was ashamed of it at the time, because the way I dressed marked me as different to my peers, but looking back, it was this history of scavenging that formed my real interest in fashion as a space of exploration and performance. I still delight in the absurdities I find at the bottom of a bargain bin, and I relish in the space for gender play that dressing up allows me.

Some people get into fat acceptance through politics or through reading. Some people discover it through activism, events, or academia. I got into it through dressing up and particularly through finding Fatshionista and other fat-positive fashion communities online. It was through Fatshion that I was able to renegotiate my relationship to my body. I found that space at a time in my life where I was in constant struggle with my body image, swinging between crash dieting and binge eating in a vicious circle that was dramatically affecting my mental and physical health—a cycle that I'm sure I would still be in if it hadn't been for finding that space.

At the time, I was still desperate to make my body acceptable and to fit in with the suburban art students I hung out with. I'd dieted on and off for years, but never with any noticeable result. Clothes had been part of my strategy to achieve this acceptability; I watched endless makeover shows, making note of any "tips" for fat girls and basing my wardrobe selections around the many rules and regulations that I'd set in place to make sure that my fat remained as invisible as it could. I knew that my body marked me as different from others and that it garnered attention from people I didn't want to notice me.

I always endeavored to dress to flatter my shape. This, for me, was an oppressive notion based on dressing what I felt was an unacceptable body. For those years, my thighs and arms rarely saw the light of day and everything I wore skimmed over my hips, tummy, and emphasized my (admittedly fairly lacking) cleavage. I shopped with a strict set of rules, gained mainly from a teenage addiction to makeover programs, and I never tried anything that contradicted these rules. I looked good, and I won't deny, I often got complimented. I attracted the usual fatty taunts, but not nearly as many as I do now, because the way I dressed made me socially acceptable. I dressed in a way that told others that I, too, was aware of my bodily inferiority. Shopping was still fun for me, but it involved so much less spontaneity, fun, laughter, and general enjoyment, and much more scouting for pieces that would help me blend in.

Even now, I can remember the first time I saw a fat body differently. It was on a now near-defunct LiveJournal community, centered around high street fashion in the UK. It was a space that celebrated and idolized celebrity bodies and shamed fat bodies. There were fat women visible on the community, but they were only acceptable as long as they also reiterated their bodily inferiority in the outfits they chose, and in their commentary on fat celebrities such as Beth Ditto. There was one poster, however, who became visible on the community without conforming to these predesignated restrictions. I can remember her photographs to the day. It was the first time I saw a fat woman in a miniskirt in wet-look leggings and form-fitting dresses. I remember the controversy it caused among the straight-size posters and how for the first time I didn't agree with the rest of the posters. It was maybe the first time that I realized that different bodies could work one style in a variety of ways—and that was awesome. I began to rethink the mechanisms of flattery, because, whilst the clothes the poster wore looked amazing to me, they emphasized her fattest parts—her thick thighs, big behind, and chunky arms. Her dress sense didn't conform to the common goal of dressing for the other women in the community and it didn't make her look any thinner.

It was shortly afterward that I discovered the Fatshionista community, which had a more politically radical fat-positive focus. Clothes became a way to interact with my fat body. To start off with, Fatshion communities were spaces that showed me that there were other people out there with my measurements. In days when I couldn't look at myself in the mirror, Fatshionista was a source of empowering images that showed me that there was nothing wrong with my body. As a fat person, you're constantly confronted with images of fat bodies that carry the symbolism of the obesity epidemic and that tell you that you're not a person—images that are taken of us, then cropped, and resold to mainstream media. What Fatshion communities and bloggers do is counteract these images with radical alternatives, and by doing this I think we help to deconstruct the false rhetoric of those images. It's hard to continue believing that your body is a walking death sentence when you see images of other people with similar shapes who seem to be the very opposite of this!

Fatshionista taught me that there was no such thing as bad bodies or bad parts of my body. There was no need to conform to this doctrine of flattery and acceptability if I didn't see my fattest parts as inferior to the rest of me. I began to reject the rules I'd believed in and shift my focus onto a different set of role models. Flattery had been something I'd held onto for a long time, but with it always came a certain amount of compromise over my body. Growing up watching makeover shows, I'd always taken in the gospel of dressing "well" and flattering my body. These shows told me that dressing a certain way not only would make me attractive to people who would otherwise shun my body, but also was my responsibility to the people who loved me to present an image that showed "the best of me." With changing the way I dressed, I shifted my sense of responsibility onto taking care of myself for my own reasons.

Now I wear clothes as a form of resistance. I am a fat woman, and yet I have worn miniskirts, hot pants, high necklines, low necklines, pencil skirts, wiggle dresses, bustiers, corsets, short shorts, spaghetti straps, high waisted, drop waisted, muu muus, shift dresses, kaftans, see-through everything, sequins, spandex, lamé, PVC, body con dresses, jumpsuits, leggings, mesh, unitards, knee socks, dungarees, ruffles, pleating, draping, vintage dresses, skinny jeans, leather. . . . I have worn everything that I have *wanted* to wear, *regardless* . . . no, not just regardless of my body, it's more than that now. I wear the clothes I love *because* of my body—because I love the way that these things look and feel on my fat body and your fat body, because I want the world to see my tree-trunk thighs, my door-frame–wide hips, and my broad shoulders, and because I want to see a variety of body shapes and sizes in public spaces.

Don't ever decide not to wear something because you are fat. In fact, I try and do the opposite whenever I go shopping. Wear something ridiculous *because* you are fat. Wear something you *shouldn't* wear because you are fat. Now, when I shop, I try on the most absurd items in the shop, sometimes because I want to own them and sometimes just for fun. What's the worst that could happen? You laugh a bit, and put it back on the hanger. What's the best thing that could happen? You feel fantastic, sexy, and empowered, and you discover new ways to express yourself.

The only person that should tell you what you should and shouldn't wear is yourself, not external disciplinary agencies; not your friends, family, lovers; not the magazines and makeover shows; and certainly not the anonymous hater in the street (or on the Internet). Wear what you want, rather than what you're told to want. Fatshion doesn't have to be about making your body acceptable. For me, in fact, it was about acknowledging my very unacceptability as part of me and my identity. Being fat was part of my identity, and my clothes could play with this identity in a way that affirmed and accentuated this fatness.

I know that dressing the way I do is a form of resistance because of the responses I get. Refusing to be invisible as a fat woman isn't easy. People already see my body as public property, but clothe that body in a pink miniskirt and a crop top or a skintight dress, and I'm subject to even more invasion. Some people think I'm deluded and give me sage fashion advice, some are physically inappropriate with me, and many are just plain abusive. My body is politically potent, both in and out of clothes, and there's rarely a day when I am not made aware of this fact. However, it's also found me communities that support my oppression and existence as a fat woman and it's allowed me to survive and, most importantly, to find fun and pleasure in my body again.

To me, my clothes feel like armor. They form an outward shell that tells anyone who wants to that they can't fuck with me. They help me leave the house on mornings when the outside world seems unbearable. They're my best self-care mechanism. They help me hold myself together when someone shouts at me, instead of hurting for days like I used to. They help insults bounce off my surface, instead of hitting me deeper than I'd like. The way I dress is an expression of both who I am and who I want to be. Dressing offers me a space to explore identities and play with facets of myself. It makes my body visible in spaces where I'm often forced to hide it. It allows me to have fun with my body in a way that I never could whilst conforming to an endless set of fashion rules.

Fashion is often held up as frivolous, conformist, unnecessary, and capitalist-engaged, within both fat-positive and feminist circles, scholarship, and activisms. While I don't deny that it can be some or all of those things, for me it's also been a survival strategy and the most important way of negotiating my relationship with my body. It's so much more than looking good or bad or fitting into dominant or subcultural aesthetics; it's become a radical political mechanism that resists the daily oppression I face and reclaims the body that I have always been told is not my own.

To you, it might just be an outfit, but to me it's performance, play, care, support, resistance, survival, and fighting.

Who Wears Short Shorts?

Margitte Kristjansson

In elementary school, I had a bully. At recess, he taunted me relentlessly, called my mother names, and generally made my life a living hell. I remember him so clearly; the thought of his serpentine smile just after delivering a "clever" one-liner about my weight sometimes makes me cringe even now. His name was Mark, and he was a year older than I. He had friends, two boys in my grade, who helpfully offered to pick on me when he couldn't. Still, if you had asked me then, I probably would have told you they were my friends. As a young girl, their attitude toward me was confusing; sometimes, I was "one of the guys"—this was mostly when we were playing kickball and I was using my glorious thunder thighs to help them score points—but mostly I was just "silicone lady[1]," "fatty," or "that girl with cellulite thighs."

I think a lot of the kids in our neighborhood looked up to Mark. He was "cool"; he was older, occasionally smoked cigarettes, and didn't care about school. I think sometimes I even sort of had a crush on Mark, as much as it pains me to admit it. So this explains in part why I was sort of excited when he and his friends happened to walk into McDonald's at the same time my girlfriends and I were ordering our McChicken sandwiches one summery Seattle day in 1996.

After ordering ("McChicken please, no tomato, extra mayonnaise, thank you!"), we sat down. I remember that it was uncharacteristically hot for Seattle in the summer, and the half-mile walk from my friend's house to the local McDonald's had me thanking my dad for making me wear shorts that day. They were new, I remember, because they were white and had no stains. The faux fringe tickled the outsides of my thighs as I sat on the end of our girls-only booth. The boys sauntered over, Mark sipping ever-so-casually from a large Coke.

"Hey fatty," he sneered. My heart sank; today I wasn't going to be one of the guys or even that girl with big tits. Today I was just fat.

"Don't call me that," I said as pointedly as I could. Although I was hurt, I was never one to be shy about my anger.

"Didn't anyone ever tell you not to wear shorts? Damn you look sooooo ugly in those shorts, fatty."

"Shut *up*, Mark." My face started to get hot and my upper chest a deep blotchy red.

He bent down so that we were at eye level and as if we were intimately involved he cooed softly, "Your thighs are so full of cellulite. You are so *gross*, fatty."

That next summer, even though Mark was long gone, I didn't dare wear shorts.

Sadly, it took way too long for his condemnation of fat-girls-in-shorts to fade from my memory. And even when it did several years later, I still couldn't bring myself to wear shorts. Only then, in high school, I was convinced it was because I hated my knees.

I *hated* my knees.

They were dimpled and lacking any kind of kneecap definition. The backs of them were covered in faded stretch marks from that time in sixth grade when I grew two inches in a matter of months. Who could ever love a girl with such chubby nonknees?

I wore skirts with tights, or they were long enough to disguise my upper-leg region even if I was sitting down. Mostly, I wore pants, even in the summer, even at the beach. For the longest time, only my closest friends saw the area between my belly and my calves. My dad—the most loving dad I've known and yet the very same man that put me on my first diet at nine—was at an utter loss. No matter what he said to me, no matter how silly he said I was being, he never got me into another pair of shorts.

"No one *cares* about your legs, honey! You look like you're dying in those jeans. Come on, just buy one pair?"

And I knew, somewhere in the back of my head, that he was totally right. But I just couldn't bring myself to do it.

In my senior year of high school, I was on the homecoming court. Everyone was required to wear black formalwear; my fellow duchesses and our queen all chose cute cocktail-style dresses. I wore a long, gorgeous velvet gown with a sparkly rhinestone trim around the bust. It was a beautiful dress, but its primary draw was that it covered my fat legs right up. *Nothing to see here, no cellulite in sight, please move along.*

My partners all begged me to get over my fear of shorts, but the closest I got was a heat-friendly pair of seersucker Bermudas that, owing to my short stature, grazed the tops of my knees so that they were at least partially hidden from view.

I remember that old Nair commercial. Some carefree white girl, tan and toned, frolics on the beach in her bikini top and light blue jean cutoffs. "Who wears short shorts?" the chorus asks. "If you dare wear short shorts, Nair for short shorts!" This is what that and similar advertisements taught younger-me: Pretty girls who are definitely not fat and whose legs are definitely not hairy get to wear short shorts. The rest of us are shit out of luck.

One summer in Seattle, when I was in college, a group of my friends from high school and I went to go see the fireworks show at Gasworks Park. I had just arrived home from a three-month study abroad in Italy, and my extremely mixed feelings about my body were at an all-time high. While the people in Italy generally treated me like a simultaneously revolting-yet-mesmerizing attraction, it was there where I first sunbathed topless and skinny-dipped by moonlight. I was beginning to feel really, deliciously good in my skin, and I thought it might be time to don some legitimate, non-Bermuda-style shorts for the very first time since my youth. On a whim, I bought a pair at Target and decided to wear them to Gasworks with my friends.

"Wow, I can't believe I can see your knees!" one friend remarked.

Another friend burst out laughing. "Oh my God, don't you ever shave up there? Your upper thighs are so hairy!"

I looked down, and noticed that the fine blond hairs on my thighs were glittering in the sunlight. I blushed. "My mom said I didn't need to shave up here . . ."

"Well you do." There was a pause, as my friend thought of something else to say. "I just . . . can't believe you're wearing shorts."

That experience quelled any desire I had to try shorts again for a very long time. Some years later, I ended up in San Diego, California, to pursue my PhD in communication. I was accepted to a prestigious department for my work in fat studies. I was twenty-three, a burgeoning fat activist, a soon-to-be fat studies scholar, and I still would not wear shorts. My first October in San Diego the Santa Ana winds came, and it was well over 100 degrees outside. I swam in my pool without compunction and wore pretty sundresses that allowed what little breeze there was to wind its way around my upper thighs. It felt nice, but I still wasn't ready for shorts. Somewhere in my subconscious, even though I was sure I had left elementary school bullshit behind, Mark was there, whispering terrible things about my gross, ugly thighs. How dare I wear shorts? How *dare* I?

There wasn't a magical moment where I suddenly woke up one day and decided to wear shorts again as a fat-accepting person. To be honest I can't even remember why I clicked "add to cart" when I was browsing the Old Navy web site and happened upon another pair of Bermudas, this time in pink. They were shorter than my last pair and did nothing to hide my knees or my hairy thighs. The fabric was thin, and in the right light you could see my dimpled legs in all their fatty glory. To be honest, I didn't feel entirely comfortable in them at first, but I forced myself to wear them anyway, and they started to feel normal, good. I even, on a last-minute emergency trip back home in August, brought them with me to Seattle.

"Oh my God! Oh my God!" my dad said, welcoming me home in a huge bear hug.

"What? What?!" I asked, confused by my dad's excitement. "It's just me!"

"Everyone!" he called around to the house. "She's finally wearing shorts! Thank God, Maggie is finally wearing shorts!"

He hugged me again. "You look great, sweetie."

I grinned, my face hidden in the folds of his baggy T-shirt. "Thanks Dad, I know."

And I did know it, I really did. Because even though the shorts were a little too baggy and not the most attractive length on me (Bermudas are the worst), I was so *happy* to be wearing comfortable clothing in the humid 90+ degree weather. I looked good because I felt fucking amazing.

Flash-forward six months and I'm vacationing in Mexico with my boyfriend. I'm wearing the shortest shorts I could find in the plus department at Old Navy (let's not even get started on the shitty, limited selection of hot shorts for fat folks). They are just four or five inches in length, have a faux rolled-up look to them, and are a beautiful soft baby blue. My epically proportioned ass looks awesome in them. My boyfriend can't stop talking about how much he loves my legs, about how sexy I look in short shorts. We're in bed together, me wearing the shorts, and he can't keep his fingers (or lips) off of me. And I lay there, letting him hungrily touch all of my lower body, taking care to caress the backs of my knees, to tell me how beautiful they are, to kiss his way up my rippled thighs, and to just nestle his head in between my legs, his face feeling the softness of the shorts.

And though these moments with my boyfriend are beautiful and feel so, *so* good, the best thing about my short shorts is that I don't wear them for anyone but myself.

I spent the entirety of my most recent summer in several pairs of short shorts and even shorter skirts. That amazing feeling of the breeze curling up between my thighs was mine to have all summer. And I was sad in a way I had never experienced in my life when autumn came and I could no longer wear them. Even now, I am dreaming of the heat and a chance to wear my summer clothes again, even if only for a little while.

I don't know what Mark or Anthony or their other pals are up to these days. I doubt they even remember me or what they said and did to me, and I'm sure they'd be surprised to know that I still remember them all these years later. If I saw them now, they'd probably take one look at me and marvel at how fat I've gotten since we were ten and call me even ruder things. Or it'd turn out that at least one of them was a closeted fat admirer (probably Mark), and they'd apologize for how they treated me (or probably not). The truth is, I don't really care what they're doing now. I just wish I could tell them how much I love my fat thighs and how much they can eat shit.

Who wears short shorts?

I do.

---

1. A quick and important aside, which explains how I became a feminist: I developed really early, so the boys in school often made fun of my large breasts. In fourth grade, one of Mark's cronies, Anthony, had it in his mind that "silicone lady" would be the most hilarious nickname for me. He got everyone to start calling me that, and when I lashed out at him and several of his buddies at recess—calling them "assholes"—*I* was the one who was sent to the principal's office and forced to apologize. My male principal did not seem to understand the implications of elementary school boys learning early on that it's okay to

shame a woman because of her body—and especially make comments about body parts that are oversexualized in the first place—but he knew damn well that it was important for me to "act like a lady" and refrain from cursing . . . fuck that.

Something Fabulous to Wear

Margaret Howie

I can see into my wardrobe when I wake up. The door is held open with piles of books, unfinished craft projects, and last week's outfits all flung up against it. With a little effort, I could probably get it closed. But I like the view. There's a long row of dresses in there, some jackets, scarves, and leggings poking out, and even a pair of jeans. Like everything else in there, they fit me fine.

When I was a teenager, my wardrobe was double the size. Things went into its dark embrace and stayed there, more or less forever. I rarely bothered to open it, as all my wearable clothes were stacked in my room. I didn't need the extra storage space because I wore the same thing for five years.

Due to my rigorous avoidance of reflective surfaces, I can't easily remember how I looked during my high school years in the 1990s. But I can recall exactly how I felt. The weight of the home-made needlecord skirt, or the saggy elasticized droop of the gray marl one, or that puzzling number that came in orange faux suede hung down to my ankles. All of them came with waistbands that shuffled around me in a counterclockwise direction, as if insisting that I should've turned left at some point. No matter how many times I retucked my shirts, they chewed them up and spat out the hems. So I took to wearing all my tops in a loose tunic style. I had a couple with buttons that gaped over my boobage area and a brown sateen smock that was too long in the arms yet refused to lie flat over my hips. Rounding out my collection were the boat necks that tucked themselves reassuringly high up against my clavicle, unlike the v-necks that my more devout friends suspected might be kind of slutty.

Over the wide block-shaped skirt and the high-necked, long-sleeved shirts, I would have on my trusty patchwork suede jacket. There was a buttery golden patch under one arm, a scrap of how it had looked back in the 1970s, but by the time we came to know each other, it was mottled with greasy spots and the collar curled up unevenly. It had been part of a clothes donation made to my mother's hospital, which I had held back for a fancy dress. At thirteen, I wore it to a drama class rehearsal and one of the other girls in my school had said it was cool. That was it for the two of us. I never took it off, no matter how hot or wet the weather was, for the rest of my high school career.

There was enough for some variations in what I put on to face the world each day, but it was a uniform in the way it made me feel. Cloaked from wrist to ankle, I was convinced that I couldn't manage any better. Every day I was terrified that someone would make a comment about my clothes. I knew it was indefensible, that in the allowable spectrum of teenage sartorial disorder only so much dysfunction could be played off as individuality. I knew I had no defense for any bully who wanted to make an issue of how I looked, because I was already so ashamed of it.

Only twice did it come up, both from friends, who I believe never intended to be cruel, even in high school where cruelty constantly threatens to ambush anyone. I was walking upstairs, my skirt with only so much wriggle room to accommodate steps, when one of the clump of girls around me asked, "Don't you have something else to wear?" I managed to come up with some bullshit answer, thankful that the question had been posed in the relative privacy of my micro-group of friends. The second time was more devastating, as it was said inside a classroom, a classroom containing actual human boys, who were in earshot when someone sitting behind me admired my new polyblend tunic and loudly remarked that I must find it so hard to find clothes in my size. All I remember after that was the white-hot burning rage and the sensation of my body expanding outward, growing bigger and bigger until it filled the room and engulfed everyone whole.

Nothing focuses the mind on the problem of a fat teenage female body like trying to find clothes for it. Once you've left the bedroom that you've been holed up in, listening to the Smiths and chewing the ends of your hair, you are stuck with what you have on to move through the world. Dressing my impossible body filled me with rage and then muted my rage with shame, because I took it for given that this was my own bucketload of failure that I deserved to carry, filled with yards of mock corduroy and thighs that met in the middle.

When I walked into teenage girl stores and braved the prospect of all those mirrors, it just served to remind me that I wasn't desirable at the base level of being a consumer. Even when I had money to spend, no one wanted to take it, which is rejection on a pretty big scale. It wasn't just the absence of sizes that fit, it was this feeling, like a nasty taste in the back of my mouth, that I wasn't good enough for any designer's clothes. Instead I hung out at charity shops, eyes narrowed in the search for another thigh-length tunic, or I went on solo trips to New Zealand's premier discount department store, the resonantly named Farmers. There I'd push my way through racks of maternity trousers before giving up and blowing my tiny allowance on fashion magazines. You'd think I would've worked out the intrinsic irony in this, but pre-Internet, thick glossy magazines gave some glamor to my internal landscape. They contained alternative worlds to inhabit, welcoming me in with just a cover price and small dose of self-loathing, if only I could have bundled myself in their pages and strolled around like that.

There is a specific feeling of not-belonging when you enter a boutique with your friends already knowing that all the size 18s have been snapped up or how grim it is to be shopping in a store designed for women old enough to have given birth to you. I couldn't resign myself to that quite yet. It was around the time I began to ditch the magazines for reading fatshion blogs that I found the same conviction and defiance repeated in other people's voices, and my sense of what was possible began to expand.

One day, I read a blog entry by Wendy McClure called "Fits Like Teen Spirit," which addressed criticism of a new plus-size clothing line aimed at teenage girls. The concerns being aired were that excessive self-esteem in obese teenagers would lead inexorably to further bad health. McClure's eloquent take figured out that the source of anxiety was likely to be less about encouraging weight gain and more about the cultural investment in a certain body type and look. She lifted up some empty phrases about the potential public danger of fat girls in mini-dresses and showed the aggression hidden underneath. Weren't people really worried that, as she put it, "really, hot young white chicks are among our most precious national resources, and without them America's reality shows and porn would suffer."

The part that made me tap the monitor with frantic agreement was her description of what it was like back when there was nowhere like Torrid for a teenage girl to go to find clothes and how she daydreamed of passing as a guy just so she could deal with getting dressed for school. This is damn right, I thought. There was nothing for us to wear, right at the age when you're first beginning to work out what your body means and who you are in it. That's enough material to kick off a who-the-hell-cares-I-won't-bother attitude toward clothing for years. I can see how it gets sustained in my mother, who loathes going shopping and lives in a collection of aged fleece items that she pulls at despondently and says, "Well, it'll do for another year."

In the difference between dressing like you don't care and dressing like you don't give a fuck, there was a lot of ground for me to cover. I was embarrassed not to have worked it out before. Why did I spend so long thinking about problem areas? When Beth Ditto was pissing on the rules of fashion in magazine pages worldwide, I was still weeding my underwear drawer of control briefs that threatened to cut off circulation in my legs. My first move was to resolve not to wear things that hurt. Whether it was the perpetual red line of fury that looped under my boobs, or the zip gnawing a little grudge mark into my waist, or the burning chub rub where the pantyhose gave way, I fought against it with softness.

Turning my attention to clothes, and away from fashion, didn't leave me stranded in the hinterland of purely utilitarian clothing that I had feared. With my hand held by plenty of bloggers, writers, and designers, I saved myself from dressing to suit people who didn't like me in the first place. Don't buy stuff, I decided, from people who hate you. Don't take their advice on what looks good or what exactly a problem area is. How about I try not to think about any bit of my body as a problem area? Especially since I'm stuck with it for the rest of my mortal span, which promises to be a tad longer than the popularity of whatever trousers we're supposed to be wearing right now.

The more reading I did, the further it took me from bitching about plus-size clothing issues to becoming more clued up about the fat acceptance movement. Fatshion was for me, like many chubsters, a gateway to a larger community and a more active, integrated feminist practice in my life. There has been a lot of soul-searching and ideological re-evaluation involved.

There has also been a lot of eBay.

Speaking of problem areas, dresses are beginning to become a bit of a difficulty. The situation isn't critical, but I have one for every day of a fortnight, and barely any of them come in slimming black. They're mostly pink or orange, or floral, or part of the extensive polka-dot division. Some are tight on me, displaying no consideration of hiding my belly at all, and at least one is so bright it made my boss reel back in shock: "Good God. That's the reddest thing I have ever seen."

The more radical I've gotten, the better I've dressed. I doubt that it's to do with any inherent styling ability emerging or even learning much more about what suits me. It's more to do with the introduction of a lick of fearlessness into my life. Clothes don't pull me down anymore, and now I fear no waistband.

The wardrobe in my room is a box full of things I can wear. It's not a huge space, but it's one that I've created and cared for. Now I don't look to it for solutions. Instead of trying to solve the problem of my body every day, I try to find reasons to be excited about it. Having something fabulous to wear rarely changes the world, but it's always a good enough reason to get out of bed.

1. Wendy McClure, "Fits Like Teen Spirit," June 2005, http://www.wendymc-clure.net/2005/04/fits-like-teen-spirit/.

Flagrantly Fat and Fucking Fabulous

Lexi Biermann

I love being a woman of size.

Let me repeat that: I LOVE being a woman of size.

This is not an easy attitude to have when society so actively works to make fat people feel ashamed and filled with self-hatred for their *obvious* lack of personal control. What follows is my journey to loving myself, and others, because love is really the cornerstone to my big fat story.

My journey to fat self-acceptance and love has been a long and ever-evolving one. I was lucky to have grown up in Bermuda in a house where I was not shamed for my weight, and this comforting environment was the core to my being able to develop a solid self-identity as a beautiful, FAT person. This made going out into the world of fatphobia a little easier as it could never penetrate deeply enough into my sense of self to make me loathe the way I was. My mother has always been a thin woman but never once made me feel like her body type was the ideal or that I should punish myself into having it. That being said, the world around me was saying it loud and clear. I struggled with trying to understand all of the conflicting messages about who I was and how I should be, but it was my mother's clear and soothing voice that always rang the truest. I owe a lot of my foundations of good self-image to the bricks and mortar of good love at an early age.

What I found interesting, and very challenging, was how to open up feeling good about who I was to incorporate the growing feelings of wanting to be sexy and sexual. What does it mean for big women to be sexy? Can we even try? Flip open any magazine, and it is clear who is allowed by society to be sexy, have pleasure, and enjoy themselves: thin people. For me this was a pivotal moment: Do I change to fit in or fight to make a new space? I chose to take a sledgehammer to that shit.

Most people I have talked to, both fat and thin, are at least a little surprised that I did not find it hard to date as a woman of size. Throughout my teenage years, I had numerous boyfriends, and even a girlfriend. The most important part of those tumultuous years was not settling for the sake of being with someone. I had a few boys inform me that I should be happy to engage with them sexually because they were doing me the great and magnanimous favor of paying attention to me. I informed them back, with my foot to their jewels, that I would rather die a virgin than settle for the immature rutting of boys and betray myself in the process.

For me, self-love as a big woman is knowing, wholeheartedly, that you deserve the world, even if the world disagrees with you. Ladies, confidence is the sexiest thing of all no matter what numbers appear on the tag in your pants. As bigger women, we owe it to ourselves to start changing the standards of gorgeous. Are you shopping at Victoria's Secret? Probably not. Do you deserve to feel just as sexy and fuckable as those models? Hell yes, and you are!

My partner, and now husband, is a testament to the kind of love all bigger ladies deserve. He has been there through the ups and downs of life, as well as the ups and downs of the scale, with warmth and support. He treats me with the dignity, love, and respect I deserve as a human. I have many friends of size who settle for partnerships far beneath their value for the sake of getting taken off the market. We are women, sisters, wives, mothers, daughters, but most importantly, we are worth it. Having the love of yourself and an amazing person (if you seek it) does wonders for repairing the constant onslaught of negative and damaging messages floating around out there.

That's all well and good, you might say, but what about the sex? This is definitely something that can be a dicey issue for women of size, and for me personally. Feeling hot and sexy in your clothes and out in public is one thing, getting naked and getting busy is a whole different kettle of fish . . . mmmm fish. As a woman who considers herself one fierce fatty, I cannot lie; even I have felt the white-hot pang of fear when confronted with the threshold of letting-it-all-hang-out-there sexually.

I was seventeen and finally ready to let someone get *that* close to me. I remember thinking I was going to faint over how nervous I was to shed my protective fatshion skin and be completely naked in front of someone, other than my mirror, for the first time. I remember the sharp intake of breath as I slowly removed the very last piece, waiting for the thunderous laughter to begin, but all I heard was, "My God, so beautiful." So shocked in fact was I by this wonderful, but completely unexpected, reaction that I laughed. It was the first time I had ever been so completely relaxed with another person; he didn't care that my breasts were large or that my belly was soft and round, it was all just "beautiful."

I know many women both thick and thin who would have killed for such a great introduction into the world of satisfying sexuality, but being a big woman I feel like it was a special triumph. Not having to look back on those memories with regret or hatred has really been a big part of crystallizing my sense of self in a positive way. I am still surprised and delighted by how much he still loves my body and sees only sexy, where others would see a ruined landscape of flaws and wasted potential.

Having covered the mind and soul, I want to talk about covering my body, specifically how fatshion has been crucial in my journey to self-love as a big woman. I love clothing, and I love dressing well. I make it my mission to only buy things that complement my rocking full figure and make me feel like the glorious fat diva I am. Nothing saddens me more than seeing a fellow woman of size wearing something that is far too small for the sake of being able to fit into it. If you looked at my closet, you would see a large range in sizes because the fit is far more important than the numbers. I have heard numerous times that I "dress so well for my weight, not at all like those other lazy slobs," and while I am sure that this is meant to be a compliment, I always bristle at the idea that one can either cheat the system and fake good fatshion or be doomed to ill-fitting slobishness. I am doing neither. I dress well because I love clothes and because of how a nice outfit makes me feel. I dress well because I am big, not in spite of it.

I have found dressing to be such an important part of understanding myself as beautiful because clothing has dramatic power to shape everything about you. From a young age, I remember watching my mother painstakingly put on her makeup, select her dynamo outfits, and match her funky and eclectic accessories. She always looked amazing, and people would literally stop what they were doing to watch her enter the room. She always said that an outfit you feel amazing in can change your whole outlook on the day. When you feel good, you look good. As I got older, and bigger, it was apparent that if in fact I was going to try to dress well I would have to work extra hard to find clothes that did the trick. Luckily, I also hit puberty when plus-size clothing was really making inroads into mainstream fashion markets.

Whenever I was in the United States, I lived in Lane Bryant and Torrid, carefully selecting everything from bras and panties to pants, skirts, and dresses to make sure they hit me in all the right places. I always feel sexiest when I am in killer clothes that show off the goods. I love putting on a gorgeous matching bra and panty set followed by clothing with fabrics that feel amazing against my skin. Just this sets up my mood for the whole day as one that will be fun, and I am sexy while having it. I want to encourage everyone, big or small, to stop looking at the tags and start buying what makes you feel good and gives you that little flutter in your panties. Fatshion has, and continues to be, one of the most important maintenance regimens to this fierce fatty's sense of self. If you know you look good no one can take that from you.

Love of the self, and others, has been the most important force in my life and has helped me immensely with creating and carrying on my self-worth as a big lady. We voluptuous vixens face a shit-load of hate in this fatphobic world with little recourse to make it stop. For me, one of the greatest defenses has been an unbreakable wall of self-love and the amazing friendships and relationships I have had along the way. We deserve to be just as happy as the smiling thin women in the magazines, but you, sister, have to reach out and take it. You may take a beating for being unapologetically fat, but the rewards are great and many if you do.

Smile, friend, you are gorgeous!

10 Tips from a New York Fatshionista

Deb Malkin & Virgie Tovar

This piece chronicles a mixed-media conversation between Deb Malkin and Virgie Tovar. Deb's words of wisdom were imparted over gruyere quesadillas and fancy margaritas at a San Francisco restaurant that overlooks the Pacific Ocean. Virgie's contribution came on a flight from San Francisco to Seattle, with a laptop and ginger ale cranberry spritzer, en route to a burlesque showcase at a spot called Rendezvous. Deb Malkin is a fashion industry insider and owner of ReDress, an online plus-size vintage and resale boutique that was also a shop she managed in Brooklyn until 2011. This conversation was transcribed and edited for Hot & Heavy.

MALKIN: Clothing is not just clothing. It's not just shit we put on our bodies so we're not walking around naked. It's the main way that we convey the message of who we are in the world. If fashion was like the alphabet and we used costuming to communicate who we are with the rest of the world, plus-size fashion and fat girls have fewer letters in the alphabet to use to be able to say who we are. We don't have all twenty-six letters. Maybe we only have thirteen. You can only say so much. We start with that disadvantage. Some people are great at riding through disadvantages and making it work and owning it and DIYing their way through it. Some people reach a disadvantage, and they just stop. It just stops them, and they can't move past it.

TOVAR: The first time I saw Deb she looked like a badass. She is a fat, busty, blonde pixie, a voluptuous Tinker Bell with loud style. She owned a store that made fat girlhood magical and chic. Racks of clothes and shop girls were her entourage. Her superpower was the ability to turn anywhere into a runway. I vowed I would see that store one day, make my fatshion pilgrimage to Brooklyn when the time was right.

MALKIN: ReDress was born out of two experiences. One was creating the Fat Girl Flea Market, which my friends and I did after the NOLOSE conference (NOLOSE, which stands for the National Organization of Lesbians of Size, hosts a yearly or biyearly conference for people of size) in 2001. Dot, the woman who had been funding NOLOSE, lost a lot of her business because of September 11, 2001. The economy took a big hit. Normally, Dot would front all the money and then get paid back so it was not very sustainable, not a real community effort. This was her personal money, and because she loved NOLOSE, she did this. So when her business suffered, she couldn't front the money for the conference anymore.

TOVAR: I heard about NOLOSE when I was in graduate school doing research on fat women and femininity. Not long after I'd begun my research, I was granted something like an "all-access fat girl pass" into a secret world that is far better than the world I was normally traversing. The NOLOSE conference was sort of the ultimate fatty slumber party/workshop mecca/fatshionista meet-up/hook-up/party down destination. I had never seen so many fat girls in bikinis and monokinis with parasols, in dresses and heels, nails painted red, lips too, floating atop the hotel pool, bellies out, double chins up, dimpled thighs wobbling free, like movie stars, like plump glorious goddesses. In 2011, NOLOSE began to be called Fatlandia. Fatlandia is a mythical place that exists for two or three days about once a year, like a little slice of heaven—if heaven were filled with chocolate, fashion shows, and boobies.

MALKIN: The Fat Girl Flea Market happened because my friends and I decided that we needed to help raise money to make NOLOSE happen because we loved this organization. So I stole the idea from the Fetish Flea, which happens every year. People would donate their old floggers and sell them, and that's how they would raise money for their group. I thought, "Let's do that for NOLOSE." My friends and I were talking about thrifting. Everyone was talking about how much thrifting sucks for fat girls in New York and how there's nowhere to go; we didn't understand why it was so bad. We were donating our clothes, but then when we would go to shop there wouldn't be any clothes to buy. We created the first Fat Girl Flea Market, and I think we raised $2,500 for NOLOSE, and it was really fun and great. Then we did it again the next year and then did it again. I think we're now in the eighth year.

I enjoy creating a container for things to happen. The Fat Girl Flea is like that because people can bring themselves wherever they are in their body-liberation journey and they can feel welcomed and comfortable. We're creating a space that's radical, and everyone is invited. They came and it had an actual effect on their lives. And all of this is embodied. People are engaging with your actual body. You're changing your clothes in front of people. People are handing you things they think would look good on you. They're looking at you collectively in a group and giving you encouragement and engaging with you in a positive way. Sometimes, those times at the Fat Girl Flea Market were the first times that girls had been in a dressing room with other people.

What we built was something very intentional and fun and crazy. You get chic clothes and meet new friends, and people relate to each other in a very real way. My favorite things have been stories that people tell me about things that they found at the Flea Market that they loved, like knowing that they got a $300 dress for $10. Once there was a woman with her two daughters, and they came into the Fat Girl Flea Market and had bought forty-five shopping bags of clothes by the time they checked out. She was able to dress herself and her kids for the entire year. That's exciting.

TOVAR: Thrifting is a delicious little part of my fat politic: It says, "I recycle. I reuse. I see the potential of that pink pencil skirt, and with that I see the potential in all the seemingly hopeless little things in the world." Thrift stores, vintage shops, swaps, and consignment stores are my second home. I'm that fat girl who gets other fat girls to try on what might have seemed impossibly small but is, in fact, perfectly, roll-accentuatingly hot. I'm the fat girl who wears bright-green tights and balloon-sleeve cardigans with fringe. Gaudy jewelry and dresses that are too small, too short, or too tight are my muses. When I think of the guiding principles of my life, they mirror the guiding principle of my thrifting philosophy: no chemise left behind.

MALKIN: It's incredibly powerful to create something that is successful on so many levels. At the last Fat Girl Flea Market we made $19,000 in eight hours. We gave away $8,000 to NOLOSE, and people just shopped and had a great time. We raise money, and the money has gone toward the scholarship fund; all the money we raise has directly helped people attend the conference. It works and it is fulfilling and exciting and successful. I'm a pragmatist when it comes to my activism. I have a belief system, and NOLOSE has been a really important foundation of that. I've met the most loving and radical and unbelievable fat activists through NOLOSE, people who are just wicked smart and take risks every day of their lives to be seen as human beings. It's incredibly inspiring and motivating, and it's changed the way I view my body. It's changed the way I experience my life as a fat person, and it's brought me to a different sense of awareness. The conference does incredible work that I believe in and so it's important for me to support it. The Flea Market was satisfying in that a radical space could have a powerful effect on so many people and raise a ton of money. And in some ways it made being a fat girl cool.

TOVAR: You know when you are in the presence of a cool fat girl. Cool fat girls often wear sunglasses or dresses or cheetah prints or all three. Cool fat girls aren't always nice, but you're allowed to admire them from afar. A cool fat girl doesn't give a fuck about whether those Daisy Dukes are "flattering." She might have a cookie in one hand and a milkshake in the other while her boyfriend holds a parasol above her, just so, and makes sure she doesn't get sunburned. I like to walk around in my apartment and act like a cool fat girl: pursed lips, limp wrist, platform heels, playing some Prince.

MALKIN: I had also worked for an online clothing store (http://www.alight.com). It was the first independent plus-size retail site on the Internet. They predated Lane Bryant, and I think that I really was hungry for something that was not virtual. I felt like New York was ready for something like that. I looked at the success of stores like Buffalo Exchange and the frustrating experience of not being able to find clothes there. Because I worked for this online store, I knew there were plenty of clothes, and the Flea Market had shown me that there is an unending second-hand supply; every year there were more and more clothes so why wouldn't there be enough clothes to do a resale store? I was really dedicated to this.

ReDress really came out of that. I thought it would also be a successful business. I took some entrepreneur classes, I took some classes at the fashion institute, and I did all of the number crunching. I thought it would be a way to do something I loved, to work for myself, and to have a container that engaged with people in a positive way.

It was really exciting to see somebody walk through the ReDress doors who could really rock it. Then we were the ones who were inspired. A woman named Audrey walked into the store one day, and nobody could speak. She was 6'0" tall and like a size 22/24 with hair that went all the way to the middle of her back. Everything about her was over the top. She walked in, and I thought she was really important whoever she was. She carried herself with gravitas. We ran around trying to help her, to make her happy. We loved shopping for her and with her. She understood her body and could look at a garment and knew whether it would work or not. She would put on the weirdest things, and they would totally work, and she would blow my mind constantly because she has to walk around in this world in this body and she's not hiding it at all. That's the difference between somebody who owns themselves: It made you want to know who she was and it made you like her. She was compelling. She entered our model search contest, and we all voted for her because she really had that ReDress quality: She was kind of larger than life and it wasn't just her size or her height. She wasn't a traditional model or even a traditional plus-size model, but she had that spirit and that sense of self that I'm jealous of. It makes me happy to be surrounded by people like that. I created the store to be around people who aren't apologetic for who they are.

The rule of the store was that everybody's body is valid. You don't walk into the store and feel like you don't belong. It was amazing to have shop girls who were politically savvy and who believed in the political aspect of what we were doing. Once a girl came in with her mom shopping for prom (isn't that such a horrible word?). This girl would have had a difficult time finding something at a store that stopped at juniors plus. Her mom clearly had no respect for her daughter's body. The daughter was buying this dress herself, and prom dresses can be expensive. We ran around the store. We went nuts to help her. We were hunting and looking through things. We were committed. We found her three amazing choices. She could have picked any one of them and would have looked amazing. The one she picked was $35, and it was such a fist pump moment. When they left, we felt like we had just done something really important.

In so many ways these experiences changed my life; they saved my life. If you think of dieting as a threat to your life, the fat acceptance movement has saved my life and my sanity and has helped make me a healthier and more whole person and not just a person with a fat body. If you're a person with a fat body who doesn't want to be fat that's all you are in a lot of ways. Because no matter what you do and what you accomplish, your "downfall" is that you're fat, and that's what you don't want to be. So in a way it's really allowed me to be a much more whole and embodied person.

TOVAR: One day I discovered that ReDress was closing, and I wished and prayed that I could visit it before it disappeared into fat girl memory. The final weekend promised an indie plus-size fashion show and a big, fat sale. I flew to New York and stayed with Zoe, a brilliant, sexy fat girl with purple streaks in her black hair who talks theory with a scholarly ease, and Arun, Zoe's love who moved from Canada to New York to be with her. We ate delicious sushi and talked nerdy together. Deb's store was in Brooklyn. When I'd lived in New York, Queens and then Manhattan had been my home. Brooklyn was new, and it was clear there was a made-in-Brooklyn renaissance taking place. I bought a pecan pie bar (proudly made in Brooklyn) after I took three hundred pictures of Deb's store, even the bathroom. There was a secret little corner in the store, a place for sharing stories and kicking up your heels, appointed with a cheetah print divan and plenty of space to revel in the intimacy of Saturday afternoon post-Bellini fat girl time or contemplate whether you really needed that too-tight "fuck me I'm fat" T-shirt (it turned out I really did need that "fuck me I'm fat" T-shirt).

The evening of the indie plus-size fashion show saw ReDress transformed into a den of Fat Girl High Society. Pink and red and polka dots. These were New York City high-fashion fatties, my absolute favorite kind. There's nothing like an uppity fatty with stilettos and a mini-dress. You always know you're in the presence of one because her raised eyebrow says, "Yes, I am this hot, and who might you be?" Her belly adds to her formidable fierceness. They drank red wine and nibbled tiny cupcakes. There were photographers, and plus-size models strutted out in tulle and lace and heels. This was another world, a world where fat girls run the show, where no beauty compares to theirs.

Tip #1: Don't style people according to fashion rules. I don't. I style them according to their own sense of self.

TOVAR: Amen. As Australian fashion designer Gisela Ramirez says: "Fuck flattering." If I had a nickel for every time somebody told me my face was too round for that haircut or that my arms looked like a stuffed sausage I'd have at least $7 by now (that's like 140 nickels, okay). I remember I had made a hair appointment at Oxenrose, a brutally hip salon in San Francisco, with the intention of asking for Bettie Page bangs. I had been told by at least four or five other stylists that this look would not work with my face, particularly because my cheeks are round and my forehead is below the apparently God-mandated height minimum for such bangs. I was internally rehearsing my bang-defense all the way to the salon. It began with a polite salutation ("Hello.") followed by my awareness of the facts ("I have consulted with other stylists on this matter and am aware that I have a too-small forehead and too-round face for Bettie Page bangs."). Then that would quickly segue into apologetics/career copout ("However, I am a burlesque performer and feel that this look will enhance the overall feel of my performances."). Then I would deal the final blow by handing her images that I had printed out on my computer and smile, in that I'm-not-willing-to-change-my-mind-but-please-be-merciful-and-don't-fuck-up-my-hair kind of way. It turned out that my stylist had no problem just giving me the bangs, and this began a love affair with bangs that did, thank you very much, work on me. There's always going to be a fashion fascist around attempting to dissuade you "for your own good," but breaking their rules gets easier with each compliment and smile you inspire for having done so. Also, if you're paying for a service you make damn sure you get what you want or just walk out with a huffy sashay. It's so fun!

Tip #2: Just having a tag that says "large" doesn't mean anything. That one garment could fit someone who's a size small up to a 3X, depending on what it's made of and how it's made.

TOVAR: Otherwise put: The tag says no, but the stretch says yes! If they didn't want a fat girl to wear it, they wouldn't have put spandex in it. Work the stretch. I can't tell you how many times I've gotten into what seemed to be an impossible fit. If it stretches, I can make it happen nine times out of ten. My closet is filled with all kinds of "unlikely" pieces: a Diane von Furstenburg size 10, a Betsey Johnson sequined mini-dress in size 8, a Saks Fifth Avenue LBD size 12. They hang alongside a Domino Dollhouse strawberry dress size 1X, a vintage sailor-inspired house dress in

2X, and even a 3X Forever 21 hound's-tooth miniskirt. Every piece (except the Domino Dollhouse dress, which was a gift from an admirer) was acquired through thrifting, swapping, or finding (yes, like on a street corner in Park Slope, Brooklyn, or Berkeley, California).

Tip #3: Know your shape, and don't hide it.

MALKIN: My pet peeve is people wearing things that are too oversized, things that are not meant to be oversized. Oversized can be a look that involves an intentionality. It can't just be oversized everywhere. People who are afraid of the contours of their body hide under clothing that is too big, and it actually makes them look bigger, and I find it also makes you feel sad because you're hiding in plain sight. And *flattering* doesn't always mean *slimming*, but *flattering* does mean that you're agreeing or conforming to a certain set of rules that you did not create about what's attractive. I believe people should wear whatever the fuck they want to wear, and if you don't want to wear a bra then don't, but own it and don't complain when the girls with cleavage get more attention.

Often a woman would come into ReDress and try on a dress that was oversized or just too big and I told her it was just "eh," and then I handed her a dress that was more form-fitting. It was this process of revealing to her that she had a body and, even if it wasn't the shape she fantasized about having, she had shape. You could see the little lightbulbs go off in people's minds. We would ask them to take risks. You can't ask women to take too many risks at one time. You can't say "wear this thing that's tight on your ass and show your arms" or "wear this thing that's low-cut, which you never ever do and have it be really short." You have to pick one, and women would come back to the store and tell me how often they went out in this dress, and it was above their knees, and they'd never shown their legs before. This older woman told me she'd never shown her legs before, and she wore this dress to a friend's wedding, and she got so many compliments.

Tip #4: There's a difference between skintight and form-fitting.

MALKIN: I don't love to have things super tight on my belly. It makes me feel less comfortable. There are places where I will wear things that I wouldn't wear everywhere. I don't feel like I need to have the freedom to wear it everywhere.

Tip #5: Know what you're comfortable with, and be willing to go one step beyond it.

MALKIN: I find fat women need permission to do things, to live their lives. I wish I could say, "You don't need permission," but I find I sometimes need that permission, too. I get very inspired by seeing what other women wear and how they do things. I think of myself as a pretty realized human being without a lot of rules, but I need that inspiration or that permission sometimes.

When I dress, I try to think about what I want to convey. I need things to be comfortable. I'm comfort-obsessed so I don't, for example, really wear heels. Some people are willing to put up with the pain for the reward. Maybe I'll wear a pair of leggings and a short miniskirt. So maybe I won't have my bare thighs out for the world to see because it will distract me from whatever the hell it is I'm there trying to enjoy. Whatever I'm wearing, a short skirt is usually a pretty big deal. I know that about myself.

Tip #6: Think about something you've always wanted to do, and find your version of that.

MALKIN: Being playful and engaging joyfully in dressing up is important.

Tip #7: Black is not slimming!

MALKIN: You're still fat even if you wear all black. Wearing all black doesn't make you disappear. It doesn't make your hips smaller. Wearing color is not going to somehow make you any more fat than you actually are. I challenge people to wear stripes and color.

Tip #8: Steal people's looks.

MALKIN: That's always a good idea! Go on some fashion blogs, find a look you really like, and just steal the whole damn thing! If you post a picture of yourself online, give them credit. They'll appreciate it. They would love to know that they inspired you.

Tip #9: Get things tailored!

MALKIN: There's not a single celebrity who buys a pair of jeans off the rack that fit perfectly. They get everything tailored. They get T-shirts tailored! They look the way they look because they alter their clothing. I have had tons of women tell me they won't get anything tailored. It is a lot to expect of a designer who's making a mass production line of clothing to have it fit your body perfectly. As we get fatter, the variety of shapes of our bodies increases. So there is more variety of shapes as we get bigger than there is for smaller people. And smaller folks don't seem to have the same hang-ups about taking something to the tailor and having it altered, but fatties seem to think it's a way of maligning their body, as if the only reason they need to get it tailored is because they're fat. I try to tell them that this is mass-market clothing and you don't have a mass-market body. You have your body. Develop a relationship with a tailor. Go buy clothes you like, and have the tailor fix them. It's less expensive than you think.

TOVAR: I'm one of those fat girls who fancies herself a fashion EMT. The components of my fat girl fatshion emergency kit are (in order of necessity): a pair of scissors, a chunky belt, safety pins, cute buttons, and a seam ripper. Scissors are absolutely required to make necklines plungier, dresses shorter, and sleeves wider. A well-planned series of snips have taken uncountable outfits from uncomfortable to irresistible and from frumpy to foxy. Chunky belts are amazing for adding shape, shortening, and adding color. My mantra: "It's got potential." I remember once I found a purple muu muu at a thrift store. It had a crew neck and was covered in little pleats. It was, in short, a mess. That dress unaltered would have cost me scowls and hisses, but the color was rich, and, girl, you can always remove fabric; it's harder to add it. I took that dress home, took one long snip down the front and finished it off with a chunky mustard yellow belt. Every time I wore that dress for the three years I had it I got dreamy, slack-jawed looks from boys before they managed to tell me I looked like a Greek goddess or something. If everything else works but the sleeves are too tight, snip down the seam on the underside of the arm or just snip those sleeves off altogether. These kinds of snips are barely noticeable if you cut along seams. Safety pins are fantastic for pinning things to your bra. If you have a stubborn dress with a collar that just won't stay down low enough for you to show off the goods, simply pin the dress to the band of your bra or the bottom of the cup for the desired exposure. Safety pins are also great for holding a seam or a button in place if you just don't have time to sew it. Buttons are just incredible for all kinds of things. You can buy them at fabric or craft stores or just rip them off of blouses that don't fit you anymore. You can take a monochrome zip-up hoodie, sew a few buttons on, and create something unique. Sew a bunch of cute, small buttons up the side of a pair of wool gloves. My favorite thing to do with buttons? Take a boring high-collared dress, cut down the front of the dress four, five, or six (or more!) inches to desired cleavage exposure, sew a brightly colored button to the top of one side, take the scissors and snip a small slit at the top of the other side, and then pop the button through the slit you just made. Voilà! You've got yourself a cute peephole dress. Seam rippers are great for ripping out the waist band of a dress and adding two or three inches to a piece that you can then belt.

MALKIN: My fat journey was born out of absolute necessity. I was in a long-term relationship, I broke up with my partner, I moved back to Los Angeles, and I started working at Babeland because I hit thirty, and I was determined to get the life I'd always wanted. I was going to say fuck you to always being on a diet, fuck you to monogamy, and just fuck your expectations of me generally. When I was younger, I was an activist. But I always felt like an outsider because I had this fat body. Some of my activism was a desire for community, to be accepted. When you're the fat girl who's dressing in clothing that makes you look forty when you're nineteen and everyone else is young and hip, it's easy to feel like an outsider. I think I was aware of fat activism, but I think I'd only gotten so far as reading about it.

When I headed back to New York, I was introduced to people like Hanne Blank who published *Big, Big Love*. That was a watershed moment. I'm leaving my apartment, bemoaning my single life, and I went to one of Hanne's events. There were all these super foxy people who were very confident. The confidence was very intoxicating. There was an element of fat liberation that was just a big turn-on. I felt like I wanted to have sex with all of the people who feel good about their bodies. I will believe them when they look at my body and tell me I'm hot. If they feel that way about their bodies and they're really confident, I will believe them because they're very convincing. There was an unashamed, unabashed, fuck-you quality that was very sexy. A large way we achieve validation is by other people finding us sexually attractive and wanting to fuck us. It doesn't mean you have to fuck them. Don't sleep with every-body who wants to sleep with you. That's a bad idea. That's the next fashion tip.

Tip #10: Just say thank you.

MALKIN: Be gracious but don't sleep with them unless you want to. Engage in things that make you feel good.

I was campaigning to go to NOLOSE to sell products for Babeland and fuck whatever it was that I was afraid of. I went to that NOLOSE, and I got a lot of attention wearing tight T-shirts. I liked that there was this whole universe of people who didn't give a rat's ass about what people thought about their bod-ies. That was shocking to me. There were folks of all sizes and ages. There were these women there who scared me. There was this older fatty wearing a fairy costume. She had this sense of freedom that she could wear something completely ridiculous. It was transcendent. She just dropped the rules of humanity, and she wore whatever the fuck she wanted to wear. I had a hoody that was zipped all the way up, and underneath I was wearing a corset. I was terrified of having cleavage that high, and I had a woman come up to me and unzip my hoody. She could see that I was completely inhibited. I wore it unzipped, and it was great, and it was really liberating and exciting and frightening. I thought, "If these women can do it, I can do it too!" I saw people who experience challenges every day that they left their homes, and I set up challenges for myself because there was no reason to hang on to that inhibition anymore. It had been made completely irrelevant by these other women who were living in their bodies. I was unbelievably grateful for it.

That's liberation. When people talk about nirvana, that's what it felt like. It felt like being hit in the head by a fat lesbian and being awakened.

Epilogue

I imagine you may be saying to yourself: I've read about body liberation, desserts, fashion, and love, and I'm ready to be a fierce fat girl now; where do I start?

Another book about fierce fat girls might leave you dangling with a sense of euphoric disorientation, with the feeling you'd been gently dropped at the entrance of a luscious forest filled with Cartier bushes and Godiva trees without a map. But this book isn't going to do that to you! The contributors have given you some of the tools in their toolkit, and I thought you might want a few more inspired by "Hate Loss Not Weight Loss," the philosophy that guides my coaching practice. I developed this practice as part of my commitment to working with people of all ages who want to relinquish shame and body hatred.

First, commit to journaling for seven days (or three days if you're new to this journaling business). For seven days, write down every single time you have a negative thought about your body. In addition to describing the thought, write down what time it

happened and what triggered the thought (e.g., "snotty coworker" or "phone conversation with my mom"). Do not read what you wrote until your seven days are up. This journal will serve as a document that will show you a few things: the frequency of your negative thoughts, the events that inspire these thoughts, and the kinds of negative thoughts you're having. This journal will act as your first roadmap. Take inventory of the events and people that trigger these thoughts, and begin to explore what it is about these things that make you feel that way. Begin to let go of things easiest to let go. Just usher them right out of your life, and if you can't get rid of them, then learn how to manage them by limiting exposure or setting boundaries. For instance, I used to love reading big glossy fashion magazines. I didn't think anything of it, but once I began to really check in with myself, I realized that the magazines *always* triggered negative thoughts about my body and my life. So, I decided I wasn't going to buy them anymore. My money was no longer going to go toward promoting something that made me feel badly. I had easily eradicated a source of negative thought patterns *and* freed up cash for little thrifting splurges.

Second, realize that obsessing about being thin is at least as unhealthy and dangerous as a doctor would tell you being fat is—and that doctor is more often than not reaching that conclusion preemptively or altogether erroneously. I used to starve myself and exercise compulsively. I had no goals and no dreams but to attain thinness. I became ill. I lost delicious meals, bits of sanity, and entire periods of my life. It was when I was average-size that I had a pathological relationship with and was obsessed with food; now I don't. There are tons of resources on the Health at Every Size (HAES) movement that you can access for free (http://www.haescommunity.org). Take an afternoon to look at the literature, and be ready to be amazed.

Third, realize that you get to choose your battles: You can choose to battle yourself, or you can choose to relinquish the people and things in your life that inspire shame and self-hate. You can choose to fight *for* your body rather than against it. If you're in the middle of an era of self-denial and self-hatred, decide that you are ready to commit to ending it and say it out loud, think it, write it down, tell a stranger as many times as you need to: "I am ready to end this era of self-denial and self-hatred right now. I am committed to ending it."

Fourth, take inventory of who is in your life. You have the right to mindfully choose people who are going to set you up for success. If you think of yourself as the boss of your life, and you think of your lovers, friends, and acquaintances as people you're choosing to help create an amazing and fun and hot life, who would you hire to help build it?

Fifth—and this one's about love and sex—please, for the love of all things sparkly, don't lose weight for love or sex. There is a myth that love is something we don't deserve if we're fat, but I've discovered a few holes in that ill-logic: (1) Thin people don't have access to a magical new world filled with brilliant, wonderful, warm people who care about what books you read and how you like your coffee. Thin people experience the same proportion of assholes and incompatibilities as fatties. As Deb Malkin once told me, just because some people have more choices, it doesn't mean they have more *good* choices. (2) Most people are attracted to a range of bodies, and to separate "fat admirers" from "regular people" is to needlessly limit your dating pool. I also have to agree with Rachel Kacenjar when she pointed out that men tend to find their lovers gorgeous and you can "never be too fat to fuck." (3) What really, really changed my mind about fat and love was when I realized that after I'd spent months nearly killing myself with mind-numbing exercise tapes that whomever my unhealthy self-belief system was attracting would expect me to *keep* living like that. That lifestyle felt like a contract I was tacitly signing, a contract that guaranteed against weight gain. And I knew that I just couldn't keep this charade going indefinitely. Call me lazy, but, girl, I just wanted to eat some damn cake.

Sixth, realize that we attract people who affirm the things we believe about ourselves. When I was a self-loathing girl, I attracted all kinds of people who made me feel like I wasn't worthy: boyfriends who gave me back-handed compliments and "friends" who put me down. When I became a fierce fat girl, I attracted all kinds of people who made me feel like I was amazing: my fiancé who never tires of reminding me I'm the most beautiful woman in the world and friends who support me in my ambitions.

Seventh, do you. You can't be anyone but you. You can't have any other body but yours. You have the freedom to do what you want with that body, but remember that loving it is a highly viable option worth considering.

Eighth, practice unapologetic ferocity in your thoughts, your words, your outfits, and your actions. Strut, sashay, snap, accessorize. Ferocity is a skill that gets better with practice, and you're allowed to "fake it 'til you make it."

Ninth, be compassionate, 'cause, girl, when you're on the path of righteous self-love there are going to be days that you want to crawl up into a ball and cry out for your mama. But as someone who has been doing this self-love, fierce fat girl thing for a while I can tell you that those days become less and less frequent and there is not one single solitary day when I wish I was back in those dark days of self-loathing.

And tenth, see the shiny, sweet, beautiful stuff that's already in your life. Open your eyes and see that you look damn good in hot pants and that you are a force with which to be reckoned.

Now that we've let you in on all the fierce fat girl secrets, you have a job to do: spread the glittery word of the coming revolution.

Acknowledgments

A thousand shared meals, moments, and people made this book possible. Thank you to every contributor for being vulnerable, for trusting me (and an untold number of strangers) with your story, for your brilliant work, and for doing it all in the name of stating the unspeakable, in the name of a burgeoning revolution that, at times, feels tenuous. You write of liberation, of joy, of love in the face of mandates that demand otherwise. Your words are guides and friends, lovers and family.

I want to thank my family for their unconditional love, despite their occasional inability to understand entirely what it is that I do besides inspire family gossip and make people very uncomfortable, and to my mother for translation services as far as this is concerned.

Thank you to Sam, for spending five years with me, for entirely understanding what I do, for not tiring of helping me vet and improve ideas, for listening to me read and re-read edits, and for having made me feel beautiful and brilliant for so long. Like this book, you are a window into radicalism, love, and the delicious freedom of fearlessness.

Thank you, Julia, for being a hard-ass and a business partner, and for being one of the first people who told me I was good at creating art.

Thank you to Dr. Esther Rothblum, an incredible fat studies scholar and mentor, who gave me advice and bought my lunch, too.

Thank you to Dr. Rita Melendez and Dr. David Frost, my committee at the Human Sexuality Studies Department at San Francisco State University, where I completed my master's research and where my commitment to fat activism began.

Thank you to Brooke Warner, the executive editor at Seal who told me once that she liked my work; these were words enough to inspire me for the entire latter half of my twenties.

About the Contributors

Erin Kilpatrick, "Shiny, Sparkly Things"
Erin Kilpatrick, aka Miss Cherry Tart, is a "delightfully delicious, devilishly sweet" Seattle femme who entertains and challenges "-isms" with fierce fashion designs, tawdry tale poetry, and glitterific burlesque. When she's not crafting fat-positive fashions through her label "Notorious Curves," she's cultivating sultry stories of debauchery or dreaming up the next bigger, gayer, more glitter-infused way to get naked on stage.

Emily Anderson, "Fat at the Gym"
Emily Anderson was born fat and raised fat in Annapolis, Maryland. A high-femme feminist and fat activist, she is a recent graduate of Grove City College, where she spread a voice of radical dissent through its hallowed conservative halls while obtaining her degree in English literature. She spent three years at Grove City as the chair of an all-women multimedia art showcase. Emily is a facial hair enthusiast, tarot card reader, and aspiring yogi. She currently lives in Indonesia teaching English as a Peace Corps volunteer. Her future is widely unplanned, but she hopes to one day settle down

with some small dogs with underbites and an advanced degree in human sexuality.

Emma Corbett Ashby, "Public Stretch Mark Announcement"

Emma Corbett Ashby, aka Goldie Dartmouth, is one of those jack-of-all-trades fat femmes who has trouble sticking to one project alone. She has performed fat queerlesque for a number of years throughout Europe and has had the pleasure of collaborating with some of the finest talent in Berlin. She is currently pursuing a master's degree in visual anthropology, where she specializes in stigma and resistance and enjoys stunning the faculty with dazzling presentations that are part theory, part performance, and part homage. Goldie has produced a documentary on fat-identified queer performers called "Go Big or Go Home." She makes films professionally and for fun; wrote a stage play that toured Europe; has been active for many years in community-building activist projects around fat, mental health, and domestic violence; and is also part of the organizer team for the Entzaubert Queer Film Festival. Goldie crafts and cooks avidly and loves to read Moomin comics and watch French Bulldog videos on YouTube. She lives in Berlin with her Greyhound, Lucas, and her French Bulldog, Bear.

Deah Schwartz, "Take off the Damn Shoe!"

Deah's fervent belief in size acceptance led to her passionate involvement. Dr. Deah Schwartz is the coauthor and actress in the NAAFA award-winning Off-Broadway show, *Leftovers, the Ups and Downs of a Compulsive Eater* and the companion "LEFTOVERS" Workbook/DVD set, a unique resource for treating eating disorders and helping people find peace with their bodies at any size. Deah is also the author of the syndicated blog, Tasty Morsels, that focuses on improving body image and changing societal definitions of health and beauty. An outspoken "New Yawker," Deah believes that it is everyone's responsibility to point out and eliminate size discrimination even when it means battling the mainstream media and the popular point of view.

Kat Urice, "To Be Seen"

Kat Urice is a twenty-something contrarian and hopeless neurotic. She makes things, arranges words, and works as an editor for Temporary Infinity Press.

Abby Weintraub, "Truce"

A few years ago, Abby Weintraub ended a ten-year partnership with Brooklyn (don't worry, it was an amicable breakup) to pursue her crush on Oakland, and the love story therein continues. She is working on a collection of short stories about illness, awkward sexual experiences, false alarms, and the like. When not busy with that, Abby spends her time cooking, sewing, and considering a massive career overhaul. She serves on the NOLOSE Board of Directors and feels damn lucky to have landed among this fat, queer, and radically thoughtful community.

Sydney Lewis, "I Came to Femme through Fat and Black"

Sydney F. Lewis is a doctoral candidate at the University of Washington where she studies Black women's cultural productions and expressions of Black female sexuality. She is also a body-positive performer. In her academic work, teaching, performance, and organizing, Sydney promotes anti-oppression and social justice. In her spare time, Sydney Lewis is a low-budget fashionista on a continuing quest for glittery and comfortable heels in all colors.

Genne Murphy, "Fat Histories, Fat Futures"

Genne Murphy is a Philadelphia native, playwright, and arts educator. Her first full-length play, *Hope Street and Other Lonely Places* (a 2011 Eugene O'Neill National Playwrights Conference finalist), received a professional production by Azuka Theatre in its 2011–12 season. Her short plays and monologues have been featured by Azuka Theatre, Flashpoint Theatre Company, MERGE at the Annenberg, Madhouse Cabaret, the Philly Fringe Festival, and LIVE at Kelly Writers House (WXPN radio). Genne is coproducer of Queer Memoir, a New York City–based storytelling series. She is also the recipient of a 2011 Leeway Foundation Art and Change grant for her work with queer youth in Philadelphia.

Amithyst Fist, "Fat Histories, Fat Futures"

Amithyst Fist is a 31-year-old fat femme living and loving in Portland, Oregon. She is a social worker who works in addictions' treatment. She has a deep passion for helping youth, queers, and fatties. She loves Pit Bulls and fighting for a better life for all. Amithyst is on the Board of Directors for NOLOSE, a vibrant community of fat queers and our allies with a shared commitment to feminist, anti-oppression ideology and action, seeking to end the oppression of fat people.

Charlotte Cooper, "Hey Sisters, Welcome to My World"

Charlotte Cooper is a motherfucker with a blog: http://obesitytimebomb.blogspot.com.

Kimberly Dark, "Big Yoga Student"

Kimberly Dark is a writer, mother, performer, and professor. She is the author of five award-winning solo performance scripts, and her poetry and prose appear in a number of publications. For more than ten years, Kimberly has inspired audiences in fancy theatres, esteemed universities, and fabulous festivals. She tours widely in North America and Europe—anywhere an audience loves a well-told story. Kimberly's shows have twice been named on *Curve* magazine's top-ten performances of the year, and in 2010, Campus Pride named her as one of twenty-five "Best of the Best" speakers and performers on college campuses.

Kimberly's work engages audiences with surprising topics. Using humor and intimacy, she reveals the contours of privilege and oppression in our daily lives. *The Evening Echo* in Cork, Ireland, says, "the balance between objectivity and intimate analysis certainly gives Dark an edge and has made her a force to be reckoned with on every level." The *Salt Lake Tribune* in Utah says, "Dark doesn't shy away from provocative, incendiary statements, but don't expect a rant. Her shows, leavened with humor, are more likely to explore how small everyday moments can inform the arc of our lives." The *High Plains Reader* in Fargo, North Dakota, says, "Dark's skill as a storyteller gets to your heart by exposing hers."

Laura Spafford, "Like a Tiara"

Laura Spafford is a San Diego native and has been active in the theater community as a performer, director and choreographer for more than 15 years. When she's not at her job as an office manager for a holistic chiropractor and nutritionist, she teaches for an after-school theater arts program with kids ages 5 to 18 and is passionate about making sure everyone, no matter their age, ability or background, has access to the arts.

Terri Elders, "Elephants Never Forget"

Terri Elders, LCSW, lives near Colville, Washington, with two dogs and three cats. She smiles at herself in the mirror every morning, whether she's gained pounds or lost some, so glad she is able to still enjoy great health in her mid-70s. Her stories have appeared in over fifty anthologies, including multiple editions of *Chicken Soup for the Soul*, *Thin Threads*, and *Cup of Comfort*. She's a cocreator for *Not Your Mother's Book*, a new anthology series from Publishing Syndicate. Terri, who received the 2006 UCLA alumni award for community service for her work internationally with the Peace Corps, currently serves as a public member of the Washington State Medical Quality Assurance Commission. You can read her blog at http://atouchoftarragon.blogspot.com or contact her at telders@hotmail.com.

Marcy Cruz, "No Really, It Isn't Me. It's You."

An avid traveler and writer and extremely happy big girl, Marcy was born and raised in New York City. She is a lover of fashion and its history, Audrey Hepburn, Coco Chanel, Grace Kelly, vintage stores, ruffles, polka dots, big floppy hats, and wearing pretty dresses. She believes that your size does not define the size of your heart or your character and that you should never be ashamed of who you are, but that you should always walk with your head high as you strut on down the runway of life. She became a freelance writer in 2009 and has written for various online publications and websites about size acceptance, self-love, and empowerment. She plans to write a memoir in 2012 about her dad and the effect he had on her life. She currently resides in New York City.

Golda Poretsky, "The Fat Queen of Speed Dating"

Golda's big, fat dream is for every plus-size woman to own her power, beauty, and body, whatever her size. She's a certified holistic health counselor and founder of Body Love Wellness, a program designed for plus-size women who are fed up with dieting and want support to stop obsessing about food and weight. Through her non-judgmental, Health at Every Size counseling programs, Golda helps women transform their relationship with food and feel gorgeous at any size. Her programs and activism work have been featured on CBS's *The Early Show*, ABC's *Nightline*, and NBC's *LX New York* and *Time Out New York*. She is also author of *Stop Dieting Now: 25 Reasons To Stop, 25 Ways To Heal*, available in softcover, Kindle, and Nook.

Tigress Osborn, "BBW Party"

Tigress Osborn is the owner of Full Figure Entertainment, a night-club promotion company for full-bodied ladies and their friends and fans of all sizes. FFE hosts nightclub parties and other events in Oakland, California. Tigress is also a diversity educator at an independent high school. She has a bachelor's degree in African-American

Studies from Smith College and a master's degree in creative writing from Mills College, both women's colleges.

Rachel Kacenjar, "2Fat2Fuck"

Rachel Kacenjar is a 29-year-old plus-size designer from Cleveland, Ohio. She started her line Sweetooth Couture in 2009 after she received several requests for fancy, modern plus-size frocks from her vintage customers at Cupcake & Cuddlebunny. A mostly self-taught designer, Rachel learned how to sew from her grandma and comes from a lineage of plus-size women who have altered their own clothing for decades. Rachel has an art therapy degree from New School University and is the director of online marketing, lead stylist, and fashion photographer for ReDress, a New York City–based plus-size clothing boutique. Her piece, "2Fat2Fuck," was written as a short screen play for *Microscopes and Megaphones*, a feminist collaborative theater experience produced by Whisper to a Scream Productions in 2010.

Alysia Angel, "Dear Sweet Body"

Alysia Angel is a working-class queer high femme. She has been previously published in *Bay Woof* magazine, *The Femme Family* 'zine, *Curve* magazine, *Salacious* magazine, and *Say Please*, a Cleis Press BDSM anthology, and she is a 2011 Lambda Literary fellow. When Alysia is not plotting her next unruly adventure, she can be found relating her life to *Little House on the Prairie* books and playing fetch with her best dog girl, Loretta Lynn. Alysia is definitely the kind of girl you bring ribs to in bed after you give her an orgasm or two, or three.

April Flores, "Voluptuous Life"

Flores is, according to her website (http://www.fattyd.com), a "muse, erotic performer, and model," but that's not even scratching the surface. A fearless BBW (Big Beautiful Woman) star with scarlet hair, proponent of the queer community, feminist, sex-positive activist, outspoken advocate of body diversity, glamorous art model, avid kink fan, and all around powerful woman, Flores might aptly be called inspirational, fat, fierce, and fabulous. April Flores, flame-haired vixen of the new porn order, is one of the most striking examples of the new sexy, from her work as a BBW adult film star to her unrepentant feminism and body-positive smashing of stereotypes.

April has graced the covers of *Bizarre* and *AVN* magazines, among others; modeled for dozens of fine-art photographers; has been featured in over ten fine-art photography books; appeared in countless adult films in every genre of the porn industry (from mainstream to queer to kinky to artsy); and spoken out about body image through her mere presence and powerful sexuality, along with her activism. April lives and creates in Los Angeles with her husband, artist Carlos Batts.

Ashley Young, "Women with Big Bellies"

Ashley is a Black feminist queer, poet, nonfiction writer, and teaching artist. She is the creator of an online writing project for women of color called Brown Girl Love (http://www.browngirllove.com) and recently completed a chapbook inspired by the project. She is a nonfiction 2011 Lambda Literary Fellow and a 2010 poetry participant of Voices of Our Nations Arts Foundation Retreat for Writers of Color. She works as a nonprofit arts administrator and is currently working on her memoir. She lives in New York City with her partner and their four cats.

Shawna Peters, "Journeying into a Fat, Fleshy Vulva"

Shawna Peters recently completed her master's of arts in the Department of Women's Studies and Feminist Research at the University of Western Ontario. She also completed her bachelor's degree with an honors double major in English language and literature and women's studies. Her final research project focused on the representation of fat girls' subjectivities in on- and offline spaces. Her research interests include fat studies, fat activism, memory studies, and queer theory, and she is currently living in Germany with her partner and writing.

Christa Trueman, "Fat on the Beach: A Mother's Battle Cry"

Christa Trueman is an unapologetic fat vegan living in Vancouver, British Columbia, Canada, with her nerdy husband and their two amazing kids. She spends most of her time trying to build and enrich her communities through her political passions. So far it seems to be working.

Kitty Stryker, "Fat Sex Works!"

Kitty Stryker is a fierce fat femme-inist splitting her time between tying people up in San Francisco alleyways and helping clients (both able-bodied and not) realize their sexual possibilities in London. In her copious free time, she's an Erotic Award winner, the host of Ladies High Tea and Pornography Society, a member of SWOP Bay, and a queer femme daddy to her boy. Kitty blogs about her professional and personal experiences at http://purrversatility.blogspot.com.

Jennifer Zarichnyj, "Dr. Strangelove, or How I Learned to Stop Worrying and Love My Fat"

Jennifer Zarichnyj (http://pussybow.tumblr.com/) is a 24-year-old bottom-heavy rabble-rouser who obsessively collects things that would be better suited for a child's playroom. Currently stationed in an attic in New Jersey, she's itching to save up enough money to move across the river to Brooklyn. She has her bachelor's degree in English writing, so as you might expect, her typical day-to-day includes sending resumes out to job scammers on Craigslist and eating the same exact sandwich from the same exact grocery store—all in full makeup and hair. On Tuesdays, she contributes an advice column to Girl Guts (http://girl-guts.com/), where she helps hopeless romantics talk to boys and gives advice she hopes works out better for them than it did her. After she hoards herself into a pile of glitter skulls from Michael's, the Internet will forever remember her as "that Halloweenie who told us about Milk of Magnesia for oily skin."

Tasha Fierce, "Inside Out"

Tasha Fierce is a writer, sex-positive feminist of color, queer femme, unabashed fat chick, and Los Angeles native. Her work has appeared in the anthology *White Riot: Punk Rock and the Politics of Race*, as well as *Bitch* magazine, *Corset* magazine, *Jezebel*, the *Huffington Post*, Racialicious, Feministe, *Clutch* magazine, and Shapely Prose, among other publications both online and off. She has been interviewed by Pacifica Radio, Jezebel, and Vibe Vixen on race, body image, and sexuality. Her website, Sex and the Fat Girl, is devoted to fat, sex, politics, and body image and can be found at http://www.sexandthefatgirl.com. She is currently editing an anthology on women of color and body image entitled *Occupied Bodies: Women of Color Speak on Self-Image*.

Jessica Judd, "Blue Pants"

Jessica Erin Judd is a long-time dancer and current co-artistic director of the Phat Fly Girls, Big Moves' resident size-positive dance company. A research analyst in a former life, Jessica is now a free-range fat activist and stay-at-home mother of two. When not dancing, Jessica can be found photographing insects, collecting crazy vintage cookbooks, fighting her cat for space on the yoga mat, and finding new and exciting ways to fight fat hatred and promote body liberation.

Kirsty Fife, "On Dressing Up: A Story of Fatshion Resistance"

Kirsty Fife is a fat-positive fashion blogger and excessive dresser located in Yorkshire, United Kingdom. An avid vintage enthusiast and DIY seamstress with a love for all things thrifted, handmade, or on a sale rail, she set up her blog Fatty Unbound in 2009, after becoming frustrated with the lack of budget-friendly, body-positive, and politically conscious fat fashion blogs. With her blog, she aims to challenge bodily hierarchies and notions of privilege within mainstream fashion circles through a mixture of outfits, strategies, craft tutorials, and personal histories, all designed to normalize fat bodies and celebrate body diversity in fashion and beyond.

Margitte Kristjansson, "Who Wears Short Shorts?"

Margitte Kristjansson is a PhD student, fat activist, blogger, and filmmaker. She resides in San Diego, California, with her partner, Chris, and their cat, Sugar.

At the University of California, San Diego, Department of Communication, Margitte's work is focused primarily on fat fashion, fat consumption practices, and the queerness of fat embodiment. Her other research interests include fat activism, histories of body regulation, articulating fat culture, and uncovering anti-fat biases in media representations of the fat body.

As an activist, Margitte is dedicated to radical, body-positive politics and community-building, online and in real life. She generally aligns herself with queer, anti-racist feminism and believes that it is crucial (and most fruitful) to examine fat identity at its intersections.

Margitte's academic blog can be found at www.margitteleah .com, while her more personal and activist-oriented tumblr can be accessed at www.riotsnotdiets.com.

Margaret Howie, "Something Fabulous to Wear"

Margaret is a subterranean bookseller living in London with antipodean vowels and a caffeine dependency. In between considering the next frock, she does subversive craft work and thinks impure thoughts about dead movie stars.

Lexi Biermann, "Flagrantly Fat and Fucking Fabulous"

Lexi Biermann is a 24-year-old fierce-as-hell fatty who grew up in Bermuda and the United States and is currently living in Canada. She has always loved her big self and has spent most of her life helping other women of size see themselves as valuable people who deserve love and respect. She currently holds a master's degree in history and is pursuing a PhD.

Deb Malkin, "10 Tips from a New York Fatshionista"

Deb is a fat, queer, cheetah-print-wearing body liberation-ist, organizer, rabble-rouser, and the owner of ReDress (http://www.redressnyc.com), an online vintage and resale boutique for women size 12 and up. Deb organized the Fat Girl Flea Market in New York, and through ReDress, she hosted parties, self-esteem and wellness workshops, readings from fat-positive books, indie-designer trunk shows, yoga classes for plus-size women, and a size-18-and-up model search in Brooklyn, where ReDress was located until 2011. A Red Hood, Brooklyn, native, Deb now lives in Oakland, California.

About the Editor

Virgie Tovar is a fat activist, sexologist and coach. She holds a master's degree in human sexuality with a focus on women and body image. Her research quickly earned her international recognition as one of the only fat studies scholars researching the intersections of fatness, gender and race. After teaching about body image and women's sexuality at the University of California at Berkeley, where she completed a bachelor's degree in political science in 2005, she went onto host "The Virgie Show" (CBS Radio) in San Francisco. She is certified as a sex educator, and has been voted Best Sex Writer by the San Francisco Bay *Guardian*. She has been featured on Women's Entertainment Television and many local and national radio shows. Virgie is based in San Francisco and travels worldwide to offer performances, workshops, lectures and coaching on body image, sexuality and writing. Find her online at www.virgietovar.com